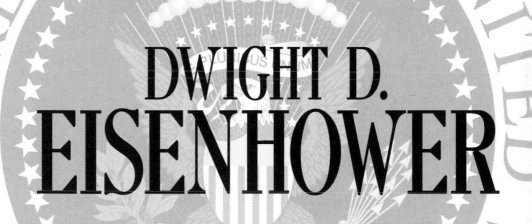

DWIGHT D.
EISENHOWER

PRESIDENTIAL ✦ LEADERS

DWIGHT D. EISENHOWER

JEAN DARBY

⌐ LERNER PUBLICATIONS COMPANY/MINNEAPOLIS

Lerner Publications Company
A division of Lerner Publishing Group
241 First Avenue North
Minneapolis, MN 55401 U.S.A.

Website address: www.lernerbooks.com

Library of Congress Cataloging-in-Publication Data

Darby, Jean, 1921–
    Dwight D. Eisenhower / by Jean Darby.
        p.   cm.—(Presidential leaders)
    Includes bibliographical references (p.) and index.
    Contents: A boyhood in Abilene—West Point—A new life—World War II—Postwar career—The first term—The second term—Epilogue.
    ISBN: 0–8225–0813–3 (lib. bdg. : alk. paper)
    1. Eisenhower, Dwight D. (Dwight David), 1890–1969—Juvenile literature.
2. Presidents—United States—Biography—Juvenile literature. 3. Generals—United States—Biography—Juvenile literature. 4. United States. Army—Biography—Juvenile literature.
5. United States—Politics and government—1953–1961—Juvenile literature. [1. Eisenhower, Dwight D. (Dwight David), 1890–1969. 2. Presidents.] I. Title. II. Series.
E836.D35 2004
973.921'092—dc22   2003022591

Manufactured in the United States of America
1 2 3 4 5 6 – JR – 09 08 07 06 05 04

CONTENTS

—————— ✧ ——————

Five-star general Dwight D. Eisenhower. The rank of five-star general can only be achieved by a commanding general during wartime. Eisenhower's distinguished military record helped him win the support of the American people and the presidency.

INTRODUCTION

I Like Ike!
—1952 presidential campaign slogan

Just before Dwight D. Eisenhower began his campaign for the presidency of the United States, a March 1952 newspaper poll found him to be the most admired living American. Eisenhower was a World War II hero, a five-star general, the former president of a prestigious American university, and the supreme commander of a fourteen-country defense alliance. He loomed large in the public's imagination as the "man who won the war."

But the public did not see Eisenhower as a powerful, forbidding military genius. He was a popular figure to whom many ordinary people could relate. He was from small-town America. He was handsome, with a lopsided grin and a down-to-earth way of talking. He had met prime ministers and kings, but in news photographs, he looked most comfortable joking with young soldiers or waving to people on the street. His campaign buttons and posters proclaimed this sense of friendly familiarity: I Like Ike!

Eisenhower's wife, Mamie, was also a popular and likable figure. Although she had never been in the public eye before the 1952 campaign, she joked easily with newspaper reporters and greeted large crowds with enthusiasm. Like her husband, she was someone to whom many Americans could relate. Many American women especially saw themselves in Mamie—like them, she was a busy homemaker, mother, and wife. Her popularity with women voters became so closely associated with Eisenhower's campaign that she had her own buttons and posters.

——————————————— ◇ ———————————————

President Eisenhower (far right) with his family in the 1950s. His honorable war record and devotion to family made him a comforting father figure to American voters.

For a country just recovering from years of economic hardship and war, the Eisenhowers seemed to reflect stability and security. Personally, they seemed to reflect values of the period: traditional family life, honesty, and likability.

In his bid for the presidency, Eisenhower wanted to be accessible to voters. He wanted to know their concerns and ideas. He and Mamie took a train throughout the southern United States, stopping at hundreds of small towns to talk to people. But Eisenhower did not limit his visibility to old-fashioned tours. He also made use of a new phenomenon in American life: television. Eisenhower hired a New York advertising executive to help him create television ads. Called "Eisenhower Answers America," the ads showed him talking earnestly with people on the street. Broadcast before and after popular shows such as *I Love Lucy,* the ad brought Eisenhower into thousands of American living rooms.

The campaign, in both its old-fashioned informality and its newfangled efficiency, was a success. Eisenhower won the election by a healthy margin of votes, and on January 20, 1953, he was sworn in as the thirty-fourth president of the United States.

CHAPTER ONE

A BOYHOOD IN ABILENE

There was bred into us [the Eisenhower family]
a certain independence and a determination
to rise above our humble beginnings and try
to someday amount to something.
—Edgar Eisenhower, Dwight's brother

David Dwight Eisenhower was born in Denison, Texas, on October 14, 1890. He was named for his father, David, but his mother, Ida, decided that he would be called Dwight. Dwight was David and Ida's third son, after Arthur and Edgar. When Dwight was one year old, the family moved to Abilene, Kansas. The rest of the Eisenhower children were born in Abilene—four boys named Roy, Paul (who died in infancy), Earl, and Milton.

Just a few decades earlier, Abilene had been part of the Wild West. One of Kansas's rough-and-tumble cattle towns, Abilene was filled with cowboys, gunslingers, gamblers, and cattle rustlers. Saloons were plentiful, and shootouts and

*Eisenhower grew up in Abilene, Kansas. The town
was a cattle center until the 1880s.*

street fights were common. But by the 1880s, the cattle
drives had ended, and Abilene settled down. By the time
the Eisenhowers moved into town, it was a quiet community of about 4,000 people.

Some qualities of the frontier spirit remained, such as a
respect for hard work and self-sufficiency. Young children
worked around the house, while older kids found odd jobs
around the neighborhood. Teenagers worked regular jobs.
The city ran the school, but families took care of their own
sick and elderly. There were few taxes and no government
services. Citizens policed themselves. Sometimes it seemed
that the only contact with the outside world was the train
that brought goods from the East Coast.

Doctors, lawyers, and successful business owners lived
with their families on the north side of Abilene's railroad
tracks. Dwight's family lived on the south side, with other
families who had less money. As a child, Dwight did not
understand the difference between the neighborhoods.

He did not realize his family was poor. He just knew that the Eisenhowers were respected in the community. They paid their bills on time, read the Bible, and went to church.

A HARD WORKER

Dwight did all he could to help his family make ends meet. He sold vegetables from the family garden, going from door to door in the summer dust and heat. He often stopped to watch other neighborhood boys playing baseball, but he never lingered for long. He knew there were other chores waiting at home.

Sometimes Dwight helped out in the Belle Springs Creamery, the dairy where his father worked. He and his brothers also took care of chickens, ducks, pigs, rabbits, a

(From left to right) *Dwight, Edgar, Earl, Roy, and Arthur Eisenhower outside their family home in Abilene, Kansas*

The Eisenhower family (back row from left to right)—*Dwight, Edgar, Earl, Arthur, Roy, and* (front from left to right) *David, Milton, and Ida*

horse, and two cows. The boys picked cherries, apples, pears, and grapes from their orchard. Their mother canned some fruit and dried some in the attic. She also baked bread in a wood-burning stove.

David Eisenhower worked hard for his family, but he was a solemn man. He had little to say and did not have much of a sense of humor. But Ida Eisenhower was a happy person with a quick laugh. Nevertheless, she disciplined her boys and was determined that they would know the value of hard work. She taught each to cook and to clean the house.

A STUBBORN STREAK

The Eisenhower boys were not always well behaved. Dwight and Edgar often fought. Out in the backyard, they rolled in the dirt and pounded on each other. Ida often just ignored them. She felt that it was healthier to let the boys "get it out of their system." But Dwight had inherited his father's quick temper and stubbornness. He often had a lot to get out of his system.

One day after school, Dwight was drawn into a fight with a classmate, Wesley Merrifield. Wesley was bigger than Dwight, but Dwight would not back down. "Neither of us had the courage to say, I won't fight," Dwight recalled. A crowd gathered as the boys wrestled for more than an hour. They both had bloody noses, cut lips, and battered ears. Their eyes were nearly swollen shut. Neither boy was winning the fight, but neither would give up. They stopped only after they were too tired to fight anymore.

Another family story involves a Halloween night when Dwight was ten years old. Edgar and Arthur were getting

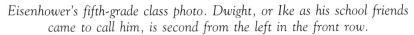

Eisenhower's fifth-grade class photo. Dwight, or Ike as his school friends came to call him, is second from the left in the front row.

ready to go trick-or-treating. Dwight begged to go along, but his father told him he was too young. Dwight's face grew red with anger. He ran out of the house, slamming the door behind him. In the yard, he pounded his fists against the trunk of an apple tree. His father thought Dwight would wear himself out with his tantrum, but Dwight cried and hit the tree until his hands began bleeding. Dwight's father finally stopped Dwight and ordered him to go to bed.

Dwight ran to his room and threw himself on the bed, sobbing into his pillow. After a while, his mother came and sat beside him. She put ointment on his hands and bandaged them. She said, "He that conquereth his own soul is greater than he who taketh a city." She pointed out that his temper tantrum had not changed anything and that he had only hurt himself. Later, Dwight wrote, "I have always looked back on that conversation as one of the most valuable moments of my life."

IKE

Although his mother did not like nicknames, Dwight soon became "Ike" to his friends. Ike's easygoing smile became his trademark. He still had his quick temper and a stubborn streak, but he was well liked and had many friends. He was good at hunting, fishing, cooking, and card playing. He also loved to study military history, reading about how famous battles were fought. He borrowed many books from the town's newspaper editor. But beyond studying history, Ike did not put much effort into his schoolwork. Instead, he concentrated on school sports, especially football and baseball.

During his freshman year in high school, Ike fell and scraped his knee while playing catch. The next day, his leg was swollen and discolored. The scrape on his knee had become infected. When he became feverish, his parents called the local physician.

Dr. Conklin treated the sore, but he could not control the infection nor bring Ike's fever down. Ike's mother could only hold his hand and bathe his head with cool water as he slipped in and out of a feverish sleep.

One morning, Ike woke up enough to hear Dr. Conklin tell David and Ida that Ike's leg would have to be amputated, or cut off. There was no other way to stop the infection. But to Ike, the thought of being crippled for the rest of his life was more terrifying than the infection. He begged his parents to give the infection more time to subside on its own. Then Ike called Edgar into his room. He pleaded with his brother to make sure the doctor would not amputate while he was unconscious.

Edgar dutifully stood guard outside Ike's room, even sleeping in the doorway at night. David and Ida, too, obeyed Ike's wishes. Dr. Conklin thought the family's reckless behavior would kill Ike. But by the end of the second week, Ike's fever began to drop. The swelling, redness, and pain disappeared. Ike fully recovered.

A FREE EDUCATION

In May 1909, Ike graduated from Abilene High School. Both Ike and Edgar wanted to go on to college. Edgar wanted to go to the University of Michigan to study law. But David did not believe that being a lawyer was an honest profession. He refused to help Edgar pay for college. So Ike and Edgar devised a plan. They agreed that Edgar would go to college the first year. Ike would work

Ike was a good athlete, playing both football and baseball. On his high school baseball team, Ike (second from right, back row) *played center field.*

hard and send Edgar money. The second year, they would change places.

In September Edgar left for college, and Ike began working at the creamery. In the days before refrigeration, Ike's job was to pull three-hundred-pound blocks of ice through the creamery to cool the milk and butter. Soon, Ike had strong muscles and a lot of stamina.

In June 1910, while Ike was still waiting for his turn to go to college, he became friends with Everett Hazlett, a grade-school classmate. Everett, whom everyone called Swede, had just returned home from boarding school. Over the summer, Swede and Ike found they had a lot in common. They shared jokes and stories about the "old days."

"He had the qualities of leadership," Swede recalled about Ike, "combined with the most likable human traits— candor, honesty, horse sense, and a keen sense of humor."

Swede and Ike talked about their futures too. One day Swede announced that he was going to the U.S. Naval Academy in Annapolis, Maryland. Swede explained that if he attended a military college, the government would pay for his education. He urged Ike to come with him.

Ike had not really considered becoming a sailor or a soldier, but he did love military history. He had also begun to think that he would never get to college if he had to pay his own way. But it was hard getting into the Naval Academy or the U.S. Military Academy in West Point, New York. Students could not just enroll. They had to score well on a competitive exam, then be appointed by a U.S. senator from their home state. Ike decided to work on getting an appointment to either academy. Swede helped him with the plans, and many people in Abilene began writing letters of support for Ike.

With the competitive exams just weeks away, Ike studied long hours every day. His work paid off. He scored second out of a group of eight. Since Ike was one year too old to enter Annapolis, Kansas senator Joseph Bristow appointed him to West Point.

OFF TO WEST POINT

The U.S. Military Academy at West Point is located in the Hudson River valley in upstate New York—a long way from Abilene, Kansas. But twenty-year-old Ike was ready to take his next big step in life. One night in June 1911, Ike came downstairs with his suitcase. His new suit did not fit very well, but he stood tall in it. His handsome face shone with excitement. Out on the porch, he shook hands with his father and brothers and kissed Ida. As he left for the train station, he turned back once to wave good-bye. After Ike was gone, his brother Milton remembered, Ida broke down in tears. It was the first time Milton had ever seen his mother cry.

At the depot, Ike waited alone on the platform. The train puffed into the station and screeched to a stop. When the conductor called "All aboard," Ike climbed up and found a seat. The train lurched forward and was soon rumbling steadily over the Kansas plains. Ike's life beyond Abilene was just beginning.

CHAPTER TWO

WEST POINT

*I suppose that if any time had been provided
to sit down and think for a moment, most
of . . . us would have taken the next train out.*

—Dwight Eisenhower, on his
first days at West Point

"Throw those shoulders back! Suck in those stomachs! Hold up your head! Pull in your chin! Do it now!"

Upperclassmen barking orders was the first thing Eisenhower heard when he arrived at West Point. The academy is the U.S. Army's training ground for officers, and discipline is instilled from the first day. Plebes, as the freshmen are called, not only enter college. They also enter army basic training.

With the other plebes, Eisenhower hurried through his first day. They ran from building to building. They picked up their uniforms, collected their bedding, and found their rooms at the Beast Barracks, their living quarters.

Second-year students, or yearlings, were in charge of
introducing the plebes to life at West Point. They were also
in charge of a school ritual called hazing. Yearlings made
the plebes recite nonsensical stories and do pointless tasks.
They called the plebes names. Nothing the plebes did was
good enough or fast enough for the yearlings. Dangerous
forms of physical hazing had been outlawed, but yearlings
could still force plebes to stand at attention for long peri-
ods of time or pretend they were swimming until their
arms ached.

The hazing was meant to toughen up the plebes and
test their ability to deal with stress. Some could not take
the harassment and soon left the academy. But others, like
Eisenhower, did not weaken or lose their tempers. To
Eisenhower, in fact, it all seemed a little silly. When con-
fronted by a red-faced yearling barking out orders,

*Cadets are run through morning calisthenics (exercise drills) at the
U.S. Military Academy at West Point, New York.*

Eisenhower (second from right) *was in the West Point Color Guard* (*keepers of school and country flags*) *during his first year at the academy.*

Eisenhower just reminded himself that he was getting a free education.

JOINING THE LONG GRAY LINE

West Point had a long and impressive history. During the American Revolution, George Washington had used Fortress West Point as his headquarters. Thomas Jefferson had established the military academy in 1802. The academy had produced many famous military leaders. Cadets were shown the rooms where Civil War heroes Ulysses S. Grant, Robert E. Lee, and William Tecumseh Sherman once slept. Instructors considered it part of the academy's duty to instill respect for the past in students. Eisenhower, with his love of military history, responded enthusiastically.

Eisenhower was much more interested in this serious side of West Point than in the yearlings' hazing. The academy's ceremonies sparked his feelings of patriotism. He was proud of its traditions and respected the values of duty and service to his country. He knew he wanted to be part of the Long Gray Line, as the uniformed cadets were called. Eisenhower committed himself to West Point's motto: Duty, Honor, Country. "From here on in," he said, "it would be the nation I was serving, not myself."

A SENSE OF HONOR

Life was inspiring at the academy, but it was also severe. The academy was nothing like the comfortable homes most of the young cadets were used to. Rooms were cold in winter and hot in summer. The food was not appetizing.

Class work could also be monotonous. There were no classroom discussions or debates. Cadets were simply expected to learn lessons and give correct answers to questions. Some of the instructors at West Point may have been good military leaders, but they were not necessarily good teachers.

One day a math instructor gave Eisenhower's class a difficult problem to solve. Eisenhower had not been listening to the instructions, so he simply figured out the problem his own way. The instructor accused Eisenhower of being dishonest by memorizing the answer. The instructor thought Eisenhower did not understand how to do the math.

Eisenhower protested the accusation. West Point's honor code states, "A cadet will not lie, cheat, steal, or tolerate those who do." Students could be expelled for even minor infractions of the code. But Eisenhower was not afraid of being expelled. He was angry that he was accused of dishonesty.

The head of the mathematics department heard about the problem. He took a look at Eisenhower's math equation. The department head then said, "Mr. Eisenhower's solution is more logical and easier than the one we've been using. . . . It will be incorporated into our procedures from now on."

AN INDEPENDENT MIND

Eisenhower was not always right. Sometimes his standing his ground had more to do with his stubborn streak. Though he liked West Point traditions, he thought some of the rules made no sense. When faced with a rule he did not like, Eisenhower often just ignored it or even flaunted it.

For example, cadets had to make their beds a certain way, fold their uniforms a certain way, and keep all their books and papers tidy. This was part of their training to be disciplined soldiers. But tidiness was not Eisenhower's strong point. He often did not keep his side of the dorm room neat and, at times, did not even try.

Every morning, cadets lined up in formation. They stood still and straight at attention while officers took roll call and inspected the cadets' uniforms. Eisenhower was often late for formation, running up at the last minute. Sometimes he did not dress properly, with various violations of West Point's uniform code.

One evening a cadet corporal named Adler ordered Eisenhower and another cadet to report to him in "full-dress coats." Adler meant for them to come in complete uniform. But as a joke, Eisenhower and his friend decided to take Adler's order literally. They showed up at Adler's room in their dress coats—and only their dress coats, with no shirts or pants. Adler's roommate burst into laughter, but Adler was not amused. He ordered the two to return fully dressed, then made them stand face to the wall for the rest of the night.

PART OF THE TEAM

Physical fitness training at West Point included team sports. The academy's football team, known as Army, was very popular. Every year, late in the fall, Army played a big game against the Naval Academy's team. It was known as the Army-Navy game, and thousands of people came to watch it.

Eisenhower was thrilled when he made the Army football team. He played hard, just as he had in high school.

———————————————— ✧ ————————————————

Eisenhower (third from left, second row) *made the Army football team at West Point.*

One day, during a game against Tufts University in Massachusetts, he twisted his knee. It was right before the Army-Navy game, and Eisenhower did not want to miss practice. He did not give his knee time to heal. Later that same week, he twisted it again jumping down off a horse. This time, he tore cartilage and tendons in the knee. The doctors spent four days straightening Eisenhower's leg before putting it in a cast. The pain was so intense that Eisenhower could not sleep.

Worse than the pain was the knowledge that his football days were over. There was even talk of him not receiving a commission (assignment) in the army. Eisenhower grew depressed. "I sure hate to feel so helpless and worthless," he wrote to his high school friend Ruby Norman.

Eisenhower's grades began to slip and his disciplinary problems worsened. He thought of resigning from West Point.

His future was still in question when he returned to Abilene for summer break in 1912. But he soon discovered he was Abilene's hero. His family and friends were very proud of him. Even Wesley Merrifield, his childhood enemy, told Eisenhower how good he looked in his uniform. The trip gave Eisenhower a boost of confidence. He returned to West Point ready to apply himself again to his grades and the academy's code.

WORLD WAR I BEGINS

As Eisenhower's cadet training progressed, he studied the subjects West Point considered most important: mathematics, geography, and science. He learned to handle a rifle and small artillery. He practiced horseback riding and studied ways to build a bridge. But his military education was not

*German infantrymen (foot soldiers) fire from a reinforced trench during
World War I. The war for Eisenhower seemed very far away.*

———————————— ✧ ————————————

limited to classroom lessons and field practice. Eisenhower
also came to understand that a good officer is highly moti-
vated and dedicated, an unselfish team player with both
physical and emotional courage.

In 1914 a war began in Europe. Great Britain, France,
Russia, and their allies fought against Germany, Austria/
Hungary, and their allies. As the conflict raged on, it became
known as the Great War (and years later, World War I),
because so many countries were involved. Reports of huge
battles with tens of thousands of deaths came from Europe.
But the United States did not want to send soldiers to fight
in an overseas conflict. The government chose to remain
neutral. So Eisenhower read the newspapers carefully, and
the war was studied in West Point's classrooms. But it all
seemed very far away.

Then, on May 7, 1915, a tragedy drew the United States closer to the conflict. A German submarine lurking in the Irish Sea sank the British passenger liner *Lusitania.* The attack killed nearly 2,000 civilians, including 128 Americans. The U.S. government warned Germany that it would not tolerate deadly actions against civilians. Americans began to wonder how the country could avoid going to war any longer.

CHAPTER THREE

A NEW LIFE

I hadn't yet fully learned the basic lesson of the military—that the proper place for a soldier is where he is ordered by his superiors.

—Dwight D. Eisenhower,
on not being sent overseas during World War I

After graduation from West Point in June 1915, Eisenhower was accepted into the infantry (foot soldiers). He was stationed at Fort Sam Houston, outside San Antonio, Texas.

While the U.S. military carefully watched the European war, Eisenhower fell into his routine at the fort. He made friends with other officers, including Leonard "Gee" Gerow and Wade Haislip. Duties at Fort Sam Houston were light, and Eisenhower and his friends often played cards and hunted.

A CHANCE MEETING

One afternoon in October 1915, Eisenhower was on inspection duty. In a freshly pressed uniform and polished boots, he set out to inspect each of the fort's guard posts. As he walked through the officers' housing, he heard some-one call his name. It was Gee Gerow, waving from the front porch of Major Hunter Harris's house.

Mrs. Harris was entertaining guests on the lawn in the autumn sunshine. Eisenhower walked over to the group, smil-ing hello to everyone. But he stopped short when he caught sight of a guest he did not know, a young woman. For a moment, Eisenhower lost track of what Mrs. Harris was say-

ing. He just stared at the pretty stranger. Then he real-ized he was being introduced to her. Miss Doud was her name.

Mamie Doud stared right back at Eisenhower. Mamie later recalled thinking, He's just about the handsomest male I have ever seen.

Eisenhower asked Mamie if she would like to walk with him on inspections.

✧ ────────────

Early in his military career, Eisenhower met and fell in love with Mamie Doud. Determined, he continued to show his interest until she would go out with him.

She did not think twice about accepting his invitation. As they walked through the fort, Mamie and Eisenhower laughed and chatted. She told him that she was from Denver, Colorado, but that her family was staying in San Antonio over the winter. As Mamie talked, Eisenhower realized that her family was wealthy and that her upbringing was very different from his own. But she was not a snob at all.

The next day, Eisenhower called Mamie and asked her to go dancing. Mamie said no, she already had a date. She had dates, in fact, for weeks to come. Mamie was very popular and always busy.

But Eisenhower was determined. Sometimes he called her two or three times a day. He often dropped by the Doud's house in San Antonio when he was off duty. If Mamie was not home, Eisenhower visited with her mother, talked history with her father, or joked around with her younger sisters. When Mamie's other dates brought her home, they would find Eisenhower sitting in the parlor with her family. Finally, after several weeks, Mamie agreed to go out with him. They began meeting regularly for dinner, dancing, or theatre shows.

Four months later, on Valentine's Day 1916, Mamie and Eisenhower became engaged. Mamie's parents liked Eisenhower, but they had doubts about the marriage. Mamie was only nineteen. She was also used to living in a large house with servants. Her parents worried that she was not prepared to live on an army base on a young officer's salary. But Mamie was determined to marry Eisenhower, and her parents finally agreed.

Mamie and Eisenhower did not have much time to plan a lavish society wedding, but Mamie did not care. She was not interested in a tailor-made wedding gown, a large

Eisenhower and Mamie Doud on their wedding day, July 1, 1916. Eisenhower would not sit down before the ceremony, because he did not want to wrinkle his uniform.

✧ ————————————

church ceremony, or an impressive reception dinner. On July 1, 1916, they were married in her parents' front parlor.

NEWLYWEDS

Eisenhower and Mamie had three rooms in the officers' housing. Mamie did not know the first thing about house-keeping. "If you don't learn to cook," her mother had advised her, "no one will ask you to do it." But Mamie was in love and anxious to be a good wife. She decorated their rooms with wedding presents and things from home. Mamie managed their finances, while Eisenhower did most of the cooking.

Mamie took charge of the couple's social life. Eisenhower had many friends, but there were some social graces he had not learned in small-town Kansas. Mamie, on the other hand, knew how to give parties. The Eisenhowers starting having friends over often to play cards, listen to music, and sing. The couple's apartment soon became known as "Club Eisenhower."

AMERICA JOINS THE WAR

While Eisenhower and Mamie settled into married life, the war in Europe raged on. Germany continued to use submarines to attack ships from Allied and neutral countries. President Woodrow Wilson finally asked Congress for a declaration of war. "It is a fearful thing to lead this great, peaceful people into war, into the most terrible and disastrous of all wars. . . . But the right is more precious than peace, and we shall fight for the things which we have always carried nearest our hearts—for democracy." It was April 2, 1917.

———————————— ◇ ————————————

President Woodrow Wilson speaks to a full Congress (House and Senate) in 1917, asking for a declaration of war against Germany.

Excitement ran high among the servicemen. No one knew what the war would bring. But Eisenhower wanted to be part of it. He had gone to West Point to be an officer. He had been trained to fight. He knew he belonged on the front line.

The army had another plan for him. Eisenhower was promoted to captain and sent to Fort Oglethorpe, Georgia, to train officer candidates. Eisenhower's assignment was important. The army was under pressure to send troops to Europe, and those troops needed trained officers. But Eisenhower wanted to go overseas himself, not prepare others to go.

Even though Eisenhower did not like his assignment, he impressed officers and trainees alike. His understanding of football helped him organize the training programs. He expected trainees to do their best as individuals but to also learn teamwork and cooperation. "Our new Captain . . . ," a trainee wrote, "is, I believe, one of the most efficient and best Army officers in the country. . . . "

There was another bright spot in Eisenhower's life. Mamie gave birth to their first son on September 24, 1917. They named him Doud Dwight and called him "Ikky."

THE TANK CORPS

After Camp Oglethorpe, Eisenhower was sent to Fort Leavenworth, Kansas, to train more officers. In the winter of 1917, he was assigned to Camp Meade, Maryland. At Camp Meade, his duties included training soldiers to use tanks, heavy armored vehicles with attached guns. Tanks were the army's newest weapon. They were a revolution in warfare, as they could be driven through gunfire into battle.

While at Camp Meade, Eisenhower met George S. Patton Jr. Eisenhower and Patton were both students and

*Lieutenant Colonel Dwight Eisenhower stands next to one
of the tanks manned by corps under his new command.*

─────────────── ◇ ───────────────

instructors at the Infantry Tank School. Patton was everything Eisenhower was not. He was from a wealthy family.
He was dramatic, outspoken, and reckless. But Eisenhower
was drawn to Patton, whom he found fascinating.

The tank training at Camp Meade earned Eisenhower a
promotion to major. When the army created its first tank
corps at Camp Colt, Pennsylvania, Eisenhower was sent to
lead it. In October 1918, he was temporarily promoted to
lieutenant colonel, making him one of the youngest lieutenant
colonels in the army. Along with his new rank came orders
for overseas duty. He was to take a tank battalion to France.

But on November 11, 1918, Germany signed an armistice, a treaty that ended World War I. Eisenhower had missed the fighting, and his rank was dropped back to major. He was glad the war was over, but he was bitterly disappointed that he had not seen action.

IKKY

After the war, the army began reducing its troops. Eisenhower worried that his career would stall. But his family life was warm and happy. He and Mamie enjoyed each other and the army social scene. And they adored three-year-old Ikky, with his blond curls and his father's grin.

✧ ————————————

Eisenhower and Mamie with their first son, Doud Dwight. Doud's nickname was Ikky.

In December 1920, Eisenhower put up a Christmas tree, and Mamie decorated it. They bought Ikky a red tricycle and set it under the tree. Mamie had been out buying more presents one day when she came home to find that Ikky was ill. Ikky's nursemaid said he was restless and had a fever. Mamie called the doctor, who said Ikky probably just had an upset stomach. But when Ikky's fever continued to rise, Mamie and Eisenhower took him to the hospital. He was diagnosed with scarlet fever, a serious infectious disease. On January 2, 1921, Ikky slipped into a coma and died.

Eisenhower and Mamie were devastated. Eisenhower was close to an emotional breakdown, but he found it difficult to talk to anyone about his feelings. He turned to his work and tried to absorb himself in a routine. Mamie was left alone in the house, where everything reminded her of her little boy. The couple never really recovered from Ikky's death. For the rest of his life, Eisenhower sent flowers to Mamie every year on the anniversary of Ikky's birthday.

PANAMA

General Fox Connor had met Eisenhower while touring Camp Meade during the war. He had been very impressed by Eisenhower and remembered him when he needed an executive officer in the fall of 1921. Conner wanted Eisenhower to accompany him to the Panama Canal Zone. The United States owned this vital waterway, which connected the Pacific Ocean and Caribbean Sea. The U.S. Army maintained a base in Panama to provide security along the canal.

Eisenhower was equally impressed by Connor. Connor was thought to be one of the army's best strategists, and Eisenhower was happy to work with him. In January 1922, Mamie and Eisenhower packed, said good-bye to friends, and left for their first foreign military service.

Eisenhower studied long hours and learned much from Conner. Together the men pored over maps and discussed battles and international relations. Conner advised Eisenhower to prepare for another coming war, and Eisenhower trusted his judgment. When the next war came, Eisenhower wanted to be ready.

Eisenhower was feeling better about his career, and life was good to the Eisenhowers in another way. Their second son, John Sheldon Doud Eisenhower, was born on August 3, 1922.

A CAREER ON THE MOVE

Eisenhower's tour of duty in Panama ended in the fall of 1924. The family first moved back to Camp Meade before Eisenhower was sent to Colorado to recruit soldiers. In 1925, on Connor's recommendation, Eisenhower was accepted at the army's Command and General Staff School at Fort Leavenworth, Kansas. The school was very competitive and the studies difficult. Students were given case studies of combat situations. They studied every detail of each situation and produced battle plans. The pressure was intense, but Eisenhower found it exciting. His strongest skills were in mastering detail and planning strategies. He graduated in 1926 at the top of a class of nearly 300.

His performance won him an appointment as an aide to General John J. Pershing in Washington, D.C. Pershing was the U.S. Army's chief of staff, or top commander. Eisenhower's job under Pershing was to prepare a history of the U.S. Army in France.

Eisenhower was granted time away from his duties with Pershing to attend the Army War College, where he again studied war strategy. In 1928 he graduated first in his class. Eisenhower began work in the office of the Assistant Secretary of War, in November 1929. In 1932, after Pershing retired, Eisenhower became the personal assistant to General Douglas MacArthur, the army's new chief of staff.

Eisenhower and Mamie did not always enjoy the routine formalities of army life in the nation's capital.

✧ ──────────────

The Eisenhowers with their second son, John, in the 1930s. John is wearing his Boy Scout uniform.

There was a rigid code of socializing with other officers and their families. It seemed to have nothing to do with getting to know people better or enjoying their company. The Eisenhowers had to pay short, stiff visits to superior officers' homes every Sunday. They were also often obliged to take large groups out to expensive dinners that they could not really afford.

But on their own time, the Eisenhowers formed a close-knit group of friends. Gee Gerow and Wade Haislip, Eisenhower's friends from Fort Sam Houston, were also assigned to posts in Washington, D.C., as was George Patton. Eisenhower's younger brother Milton worked for the Department of Agriculture. Together with their families, they often got together for golf, bridge parties, or dinners at home.

THE PHILIPPINES

In 1935 MacArthur was transferred to the Philippine Islands in the South Pacific Ocean. The United States had held authority over the Philippines' government and economy since 1901. In the 1930s, the Philippine government was preparing for independence from the United States, and the U.S. Army was helping the Philippines organize a defense force.

MacArthur wanted Eisenhower to continue as his assistant. He admired Eisenhower's mastery of detail, loyalty, and efficiency. Eisenhower was unhappy about the move, but he felt he could not pass up the opportunity. The post-war army was small, and chances for promotions were few.

Mamie refused to go at first, because she did not want to uproot John from school. But they eventually joined

Eisenhower in Manila, the Philippines' capital, in 1936, after John graduated from the eighth grade.

Mamie was not encouraged when she arrived in Manila. The Philippines were hot and humid. Heavy monsoon rains alternated with sweltering sun. The Eisenhowers' apartment was not air-conditioned. Bugs scampered across the floor, into cupboards, and up the walls. At night the family slept under nets to keep out mosquitoes. Mamie fell ill, and Eisenhower was not getting along well with MacArthur.

Eisenhower knew MacArthur was an intelligent man and a brilliant military strategist. But personally, Eisenhower found his boss vain, overly dramatic, and sometimes irrational. Eisenhower himself had a low-key personality and valued teamwork and cooperation. He found it difficult to put up with MacArthur on a daily basis.

——————————— ◆ ———————————

General MacArthur (front center) *and Eisenhower* (second from left) *arrive in Manila, Philippines, in 1936.*

One day after yet another argument with MacArthur, Eisenhower pounded his fist on the desk and demanded to be fired. But MacArthur would not do that—he needed Eisenhower. Instead of firing him, MacArthur wrote Eisenhower a letter thanking him for his "cheerful and efficient devotion." In 1936 Eisenhower was promoted to lieutenant colonel.

Eisenhower stayed in that post until 1939. At forty-nine years old, he was considered one of the best officers in the army. Concerns about his long-term military career were fading too. As the threat of war again gathered over Europe, the United States began expanding its army. Eisenhower's experience in training soldiers and commanding troops would be greatly in demand.

CHAPTER FOUR

WORLD WAR II

I hate war as only a soldier who has lived it can. . . .

—Dwight D. Eisenhower

For many years, political tension had been growing in Europe and Asia. Germany, Italy, and Japan had formed a coalition, called the Axis. Axis countries were building up large militaries to invade and take over neighboring countries. With this aggression, the Axis set itself against Allied powers, such as Great Britain, France, China, and the Soviet Union. In Asia, Japan had begun invading parts of China in 1936. In Europe, Germany's dictator and head of the Nazi party, Adolf Hitler, made his move in 1939. He sent his Nazi troops to invade Poland. The war that Fox Connor had predicted began.

After the fall of Poland, Germany set its sights on other countries. In 1940 France fell to the Nazis, and Hitler began bombing England. In 1941 Italy's dictator, Benito Mussolini, attacked Greece. Germany attacked the western Soviet Union.

Waging blitzkrieg, or "lightning war," German dictator Adolf Hitler (standing in car) *and his military rolled through Europe in 1939 and 1940.*

Hitler also invaded French-controlled North Africa. Japan continued its offensive by moving into Southeast Asia and began threatening Australia. Axis aggression had quickly become a world war.

U.S. ISOLATIONISM

Eisenhower believed it was only a matter of time before the United States would be drawn into the war. His opinions on the United States joining the war were so strong that his fellow soldiers began calling him "Alarmist Ike."

At the time, many Americans were against sending troops to war. President Franklin D. Roosevelt was greatly concerned with Axis aggression in Europe and Asia. But after the devastation of World War I, a strong strain of isolationism had surfaced in the United States. Isolationists argued against involvement in any foreign war. They said the United States should only enter a war if the country was attacked on its own soil.

On December 7, 1941, that attack came. Early on Sunday morning, the Japanese military bombed Pearl Harbor on the Hawaiian island of Oahu. Japanese planes and submarines destroyed much of the U.S. Pacific fleet anchored in the harbor. More than 2,300 people died, and about 2,000 were wounded.

In response, the United States, Canada, and Great Britain declared war on Japan on December 8, 1941. On December 9, China declared war on the Axis. Germany and Italy declared war on the United States on December 11, 1941.

WAR PLANS

On December 12, 1941, General George C. Marshall, the U.S. Army's chief of staff, summoned Eisenhower to Washington, D.C. Marshall assigned Eisenhower to the War Plans Division. Marshall wanted Eisenhower to develop a plan to protect the Philippines, China, and the Dutch East Indies (modern-day Indonesia) from Japanese attacks.

————————————— ✧

The destroyer U.S.S. Shaw erupts after a direct hit from a Japanese bomber during the attack on Pearl Harbor, Hawaii, in 1941.

British prime minister Winston Churchill also arrived in Washington, D.C., in December with his chiefs of staff. After three weeks of talks with President Roosevelt, General Marshall, and the U.S. military chiefs, a new strategy was developed. The Allies would first focus on defeating Germany. Eisenhower was reassigned to plan for the war in Europe.

Marshall had great confidence in Eisenhower. Put under enormous pressure in the War Plans Division, Eisenhower showed leadership style, clear thinking, and ability to cooperate with different types of people. His abilities brought him a wartime promotion. In March 1942, he became Major General Eisenhower.

TO ENGLAND

On June 11, 1942, Marshall appointed Eisenhower commander of the European Theater of Operations. To do this job, Eisenhower went to England. As head of the U.S. armed forces, he was a VIP (Very Important Person). Yet Eisenhower was able to communicate easily with government officials, other Allied commanders, and common soldiers. His personality and appearance were appealing, and soon even people in England were referring to him by his nickname, Ike.

Eisenhower had several close aides and was usually surrounded by guards, staff, and secretaries. An Irish woman named Kay Summersby became his driver, and their friendship grew. He adopted a pet, a small Scottish terrier named Telek. On weekends away from war business, Eisenhower lived at a country house he named Telegraph Cottage.

In spite of Eisenhower's popularity in England, his position was difficult. One of his first tasks was to improve the relations between U.S. soldiers (or GIs, as they were called) and British troops. The two forces bragged to each other and sometimes quarreled. Eisenhower understood that some rivalry between young soldiers was unavoidable. But he made it clear that he expected Allied unity. GIs would be punished for disrespecting English social rules and fighting with British soldiers.

More important, though, the British worried that the GIs were inexperienced and were not ready for the battles that lay ahead. Eisenhower feared that the Soviet Union was near collapse after repeated German attacks. A collapse on the war's eastern front would be a terrible blow to the Allies. The United States and Britain sent tanks, jeeps, and trucks to aid the Soviet army. But a second war front was needed to take pressure off the Soviet Union. U.S. troops would play an important part on that second front.

OPERATION TORCH

British prime minister Winston Churchill wanted to invade North Africa first. Taking North Africa back from the Nazis would give the Allies control over much of the Mediterranean Sea. The battle would also distract the Germans from the Soviet Union and provide the U.S. troops with real combat experience. After Allied leaders agreed to the plan, Eisenhower was put in charge of the North African campaign, called Operation Torch.

In November 1942, British and U.S. troops landed in the North African countries of Algeria and Morocco. As the Allies drove farther inland to trap German field marshal Erwin Rommel's Afrika Korps, Eisenhower began negotiations with Algeria's government, made up mostly of French collaborators with the Germans. The French colonial government offered

its help against Rommel if Eisenhower would leave it in control of Algeria. A French naval admiral and Nazi sympathizer named Jean-Francois Darlan would lead the government.

Eisenhower agreed to the French Algerians' plan. Yet he knew that leaving the French collaborationist government in place would be very unpopular with the Allies. But time was running out, and he had to make a decision. Darlan could hold the French and Arab Algerians together. The arrangement, called the "Darlan Deal," was very controversial and almost cost Eisenhower his job.

The Allies drove across North Africa. But the British and American troops were not used to fighting together, and many of the American troops were inexperienced. They encountered fierce resistance from Rommel's Afrika Korps. Some Allied officers questioned Eisenhower's leadership and experience.

Eisenhower struggled to think of a way to fix the Allied problems in the battlefield. He decided to call in new commanders for the U.S. troops. Major General George Patton and General Omar Bradley took over as battlefield commanders in March 1943. Under the skilled leadership of two generals, the tide turned for the Allies. By early May, the Allies had driven German forces out of North Africa. Allied casualties were high—more than 70,000 soldiers died—and for Eisenhower, the campaign was a hard-learned lesson.

OPERATION OVERLORD

After North Africa, Eisenhower and the Allied command began to plan for the invasion of Sicily. This large island off the coast of southern Italy was to be a launching point for the invasion of Italy. In July 1943, British and U.S. troops went ashore in Sicily. More than a month later, the Allies secured the island. In September, Eisenhower commanded the invasion of the Italian mainland.

The Allies were still fighting German and Italian troops in southern Italy when plans for a major Allied invasion of Normandy (a region in northwestern France) swung into high gear. Code-named Operation Overlord, the plans called for 150,000 Allied soldiers to cross the English Channel separating Great Britain and France to capture the heavily defended coast of Normandy. If the invasion were successful, Allied troops would establish a foothold for driving the Germans out of Western Europe. If the assault failed, the Allies might lose the war. The Allied chiefs of staff selected Eisenhower to lead the invasion. He was named Supreme Commander of the Allied Expeditionary Forces and set up headquarters in London.

British, Canadian, and U.S. troops began gathering and training in southeastern England. The Allies began amassing thousands of bombers, fighter planes, and ships. The invasion would require tens of thousands of men, landing craft, airplanes, and the cooperation of several governments. It was, as Winston Churchill said, "the most difficult and complicated operation that has ever taken place."

As D-Day (the first day of the invasion) approached, anxieties rose. Officers were nervous. Heads of government

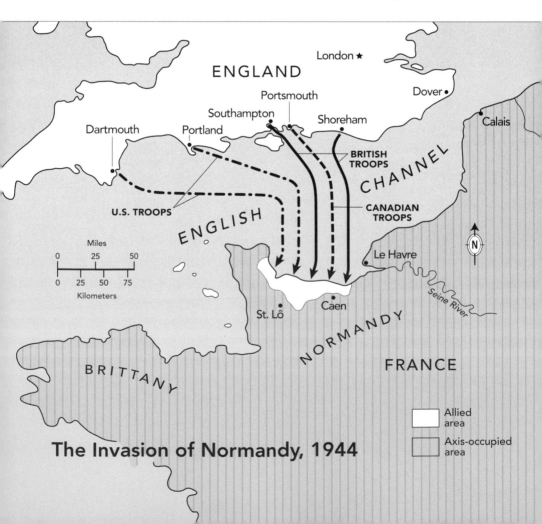

The Invasion of Normandy, 1944

quarreled. And the spring weather was so stormy that plans could not be firmly settled.

On June 4, heavy rain and high winds swept across the English Channel. The invasion was postponed. Early on June 5, Eisenhower met with his officers to discuss alternatives. The weather and tide conditions had to be just right for the invasion. Allied warplanes needed clear skies to attack German ground targets. Allied airborne troops needed clear weather to drop their paratrooper and glider units behind German lines. The tides had to be the proper depth for the thousands of troop-laden landing craft to reach Normandy's beaches. If the troop ships could not sail on June 5 or 6, they would have to wait another two weeks for the right tidal conditions to return. The Allies risked losing the advantage of a surprise attack.

On the night of June 4, weather reports predicted clear skies for June 6. Eisenhower then asked the other officers for their opinions. British Army general Bernard Montgomery and U.S. Army general Omar Bradley wanted to go. The air force generals and naval admirals wanted to wait. But only Eisenhower, as supreme commander, could make the final decision. At 4 A.M. on June 5, after listening to one last weather report, Eisenhower gave the order: "Okay, we'll go."

The next day, Eisenhower and Kay Summersby drove to Newbury, England, to watch the 101st Airborne Division prepare for their flight to Normandy. Eisenhower wandered among the men. Their faces were blackened for camouflage, and their packs, guns, and personal equipment were scattered on the ground. When they saw Eisenhower, groups of soldiers gathered around him.

Supreme Allied Commander Dwight Eisenhower (left center) *speaks with paratroopers on the brink of the D-Day invasion.*

"Don't worry," Eisenhower said. "You have the best equipment and the best leaders." A sergeant responded, "We ain't worried, General."

Just after midnight on June 6, the airborne troops began parachuting into Normandy. At dawn, thousands of U.S., British, and Canadian landing craft hit the beaches of Normandy. In some areas, troops stormed the beaches with little fighting. In other areas, the battles were intense, with thousands of casualties. But by nightfall, Allied troops had established a foothold. Tens of thousands of troops and millions of tons of equipment began to pour into northwestern France. Operation Overlord was a success.

At the end of July, Bradley and Patton's troops broke through remaining German defenses, and Allied tanks rolled through northern France. In late August, the Allies drove the Nazis from Paris. By September, after months of bitter fighting, the Allies had driven the Germans from France altogether.

Eisenhower was a hero. On December 15, 1944, he received a fifth star and a promotion to the rank of general of the army, the U.S. Army's highest rank.

BATTLE OF THE BULGE

On December 16, in his headquarters at Versailles, outside Paris, Eisenhower threw a party to celebrate his promotion, the marriage of a close aide, Mickey McKeogh, and Kay Summersby's receiving the British Empire Medal. The morning was filled with fun and laughter, but the afternoon brought bad news. The Germans had launched an attack in the forest of the Ardennes, a hilly region in southern Belgium.

──────────────── ✧ ────────────────

U.S. infantry fight their way up a road to Saint Hubert near Libin, Belgium, during the Battle of the Bulge.

The attack caught the Allies off guard and forced them to retreat. The German army pushing U.S. troops back created a bulge in the Allied front line on war maps. That gave the attack its name, the Battle of the Bulge.

Badly in need of soldiers and supplies, the Allies were beginning to panic. Eisenhower called a conference of his senior officers on December 19. They gathered in an old French army barracks, hovering near a potbellied stove. They were discouraged and tense. Trying to reassure his officers, Eisenhower opened the meeting by saying, "The present situation is to be regarded as one of opportunity for us and not of disaster. There will be only cheerful faces at this conference table."

With their advance into the Ardennes, the Germans were exposing their troops to an Allied counterattack. Eisenhower and his generals agreed that if the Allies could trap and crush the German troops in the Ardennes, they could win the war.

Eisenhower chose the town of Bastogne, Belgium, as a key point in the counterattack. He ordered the U.S. 101st Airborne Division to Bastogne to hold it. The Germans surrounded the town, but the U.S. troops stubbornly resisted. During the fighting, German commanders delivered a demand to surrender. U.S. brigadier general Anthony McAuliffe sent back a famous one-word reply: "Nuts!"

On December 26, Patton's Third Army reached Bastogne to support the 101st. But to trap the Germans, Eisenhower needed more troops. He wanted Montgomery to bring in British troops from the north, but Montgomery did not agree with the plan and did not respond. All the same, U.S. troops held back the German offensive. But as a result of Montgomery's resistance, most of the German forces escaped.

Despite these setbacks, the Allied offensive continued. In early March 1945, the British pushed into Germany, planning to cross the Rhine River in the north, while Patton crossed over in the south. The Germans ruined the plan, however, by blowing up the bridges across the Rhine behind them as they retreated. But on March 7, the U.S. First Army found one bridge still intact, at Remagen, Germany. Eisenhower ordered reinforcements into Remagen to secure and expand the bridge. The Allies rolled across Germany.

Airplanes flew, tanks rumbled, and the infantry marched over rough terrain. While the Soviets moved toward Germany from the east, the other Allied armies closed in from the north, south, and west. Canadian troops liberated

Allied troops race across the Ludendorff Bridge over the Rhine at Remagen, Germany. Previously reinforced, the bridge would not fall despite attempts by retreating Germans to destroy it.

the Netherlands. The British Second Army headed through northern Germany. Bradley's group raced eastward from the French border. In the south, Allied armies pushed toward Czechoslovakia.

SURRENDER

The German leadership knew they were doomed. On April 30, Hitler and his wife, Eva, committed suicide. The Nazi regime collapsed.

Early in the morning on May 7, 1945, Germany surrendered. It had been five years, eight months, and six days since World War II had started. With the defeat of Germany, the war in Europe had ended. Eisenhower telegraphed a message to U.S. chief of staff George Marshall. It read, "The mission of this Allied force was fulfilled at 0241 local time, May 7, 1945."

Marshall wired a reply back to Eisenhower: "You have completed your mission with the greatest victory in the history of warfare," he wrote. "You have made history, great history for the good of mankind and you have stood for all we hope for and admire in an officer of the United States Army."

——————— ✧

Commanding officers of the German military sign papers of unconditional surrender in Reims, France, in 1945.

CHAPTER FIVE

POSTWAR CAREER

*General, there is nothing that you may want
that I won't try to help you get. That definitely
and specifically includes the presidency in 1948.*

—President Harry S. Truman,
speaking to Eisenhower

"Germany has surrendered!" By radio, newspaper, and
telegram, the news raced around the world: the war in
Europe was over. People filled the streets of London and
Paris to celebrate V-E (Victory in Europe) Day. In the
United States, horns blew and whistles shrieked. In the
cities, confetti streamed down from skyscraper windows. In
small towns, people built bonfires and organized parades.

Most important, victory in Europe meant that thousands of soldiers would be coming home. Eisenhower was
not unlike the young soldiers. He told Mamie he would be
home as soon as he could. There was much work left to be
done, but there was time to celebrate.

General Eisenhower (standing at microphone) *delivers his Guildhall speech in 1945 before thousands of thankful Londoners. This was his first public speech.*

Eisenhower spent May 15, 1945, at Telegraph Cottage with his son John, Kay Summersby, Omar Bradley, and British aide Jimmy Gault. In the evening, they drove to London to see a play. When the people in the theater audience spotted Eisenhower, they shouted, "Speech! Speech!" From his box in the balcony, Eisenhower stood and said, "It's nice to be back in a country where I can *almost* speak the language." The theater thundered with applause.

Churchill invited Eisenhower to take part in a June 12 celebration at Guildhall, a six-hundred-year-old public meeting hall in London. Eisenhower had never given a speech in public. He was nervous as he stood before the crowd, but he spoke with genuine warmth. He named the differences between his humble hometown of Abilene and the great city of London. But then he spoke of how they were alike. "To preserve his freedom of worship, his equality before the law, his liberty to speak and act as he sees fit . . . a Londoner will fight. So will a citizen of Abilene." Outside the Guildhall, Londoners cheered him, shouting, "Good old Ike!" To cap the evening, he rode in a horse-drawn carriage to Buckingham Palace, where King George VI gave him a British medal, the Order of Merit.

Eisenhower treasured the goodwill he found in England, but he was looking forward to returning to the United States. In late June, he and John boarded a plane for New York. He knew he would probably have to make a speech or two in the city, but he did not think much about it on the plane. When he and John arrived in New York, however, two million people were waiting for him. In the heart of Manhattan, he wove his way through the crowd to stand on the steps of City Hall. Looking out over the sea of faces, he shook his head in disbelief. He told them, "I'm just a Kansas farmer boy who did his duty."

A HOMECOMING

Mamie and Eisenhower looked forward to spending time with each other back home in Washington, D.C. During the war, Eisenhower had grown accustomed to barking out orders and having his wishes treated as commands. Mamie was not one of his soldiers, however, and had grown used to doing things her own way. They had to make an effort to compromise.

Mamie also found that she had to share Eisenhower with the public. He appeared before Congress. He was the hero of a ticker-tape parade in New York City. Every organization, it seemed, wanted him as a guest speaker. His simplest comments to reporters' made newspaper headlines. And all over the United States, people began to say, "Eisenhower should be president."

Eisenhower felt he had had enough of being in command of people and responsible for difficult decisions. He certainly

✧ ——————————
A victorious Eisenhower waves to cheering citizens of New York City during a ticker-tape parade held in his honor in 1945.

did not want to run for president. He began to dream of retiring to a farm with Mamie or finding a small college where he could teach history. But it was not easy for the man who won the war, as he was called, to just slip away.

THE GERMAN OCCUPATION

After the war, the Allied forces remained in Germany to maintain law and order, pursue Nazi war criminals, and ensure that the Nazis did not regroup. At a conference in Yalta, a city in southern Ukraine, the Allies made further plans for the postwar Allied occupation of Germany. The United States, Great Britain, France, and the Soviet Union partitioned, or divided, Germany into four sectors. The Allies each stationed occupation troops in their sector. These sectors would be controlled by the Allies until the Germans could establish new governments in them.

The new U.S. president, Harry Truman, wanted Eisenhower to oversee the U.S. sector. Eisenhower felt it was his duty to go, so after a few weeks, he returned to Europe. In Germany he set up headquarters in Frankfurt. Eisenhower did not agree with many of the provisions of the Yalta agreement. He believed that carving up Germany among the Allies would create friction among France, Britain, and the United States, and would only serve to isolate the Communist Soviet Union. But once in charge of the U.S. occupation, he carried out the terms of the Yalta agreement.

Although Germany had been an enemy, Eisenhower knew that punishing the Germans too severely would accomplish nothing. On the contrary, a reformed and revitalized Germany could be a powerful ally in Europe.

The German economy needed to be repaired, and the German people needed to be encouraged to join in the democratic processes that would reform their government.

While Eisenhower was in Germany, the war in the Pacific was coming to an end. Allied forces pushed the Japanese back in the Pacific and were preparing for an invasion of Japan. The invasion never came. On August 6, 1945, a single U.S. B-29 plane called the *Enola Gay* dropped an atomic bomb on the Japanese city of Hiroshima. The bomb destroyed everything within a thirteen-square-mile radius. It immediately killed or injured 140,000 people.

——————————— ✧ ———————————

The Japanese city of Hiroshima stands in ruins after being hit with a single atomic bomb in 1945. While the bomb's destructive force was horrific, its use shortened the war in the South Pacific and saved more lives than it took.

A sailor and a nurse kiss at Times Square, New York City, elated by news of the Japanese surrender.
————————— ✧

Three days later, a second atomic bomb was dropped on the city of Nagasaki, Japan. On September 2, aboard the battleship *Missouri* in Tokyo Bay, the Japanese surrendered. World War II was over.

BACK TO WASHINGTON

Eisenhower returned to Washington, D.C., in November 1945 to become the U.S. Army's chief of staff. He still dreamt of retiring to a farm with Mamie, but once again that wish was set aside.

In peacetime, Eisenhower faced a different kind of battle. He fought with Congress over the size of the postwar army. Eisenhower called for a strong army. He never wanted to see another war. But as a soldier, he believed that the only way to ensure peace was to keep an army well trained and well armed.

Nevertheless, Eisenhower had to oversee the demobilization of the army, which shrank from more than 8 million men and women to fewer than 1 million. His time as the chief of staff was difficult but brief. In 1947, at the age of fifty-seven, he retired from the army as a five-star general.

NO TO POLITICS

On June 10, 1947, Eisenhower's son John married Barbara Thompson. Eisenhower was delighted to have a daughter-in-law in the family, but as always, his life was mostly taken up by outside pressures. More and more individuals and organizations were asking him to run for president in the 1948 election. Both Democrats and Republicans wanted to nominate him for the presidency. He was respected for the leadership he had shown during the war, and his honest and friendly personality made him very popular. But he insisted that he was not interested in politics. He was not even sure to which political party he belonged.

A friend from Texas wrote that he wanted to establish an "Eisenhower for President's Club." Eisenhower firmly replied that "nothing could be so distasteful to me as to engage in political activity of any kind." To his brother Edgar, he said he believed that as a soldier, he was already "at the top of any reputation I could hope to build."

But Eisenhower's feelings about politics may have been more complex. In his diary, he jokes about his firm denials about seeking the presidency. In the back of his mind, however, he writes that he was thinking that he merely needed to be "convinced I can win." Unlike his supporters, Eisenhower did not yet believe his popularity would carry him into the White House.

COLUMBIA UNIVERSITY

After retiring from the army, Eisenhower accepted a position as president of Columbia University in New York City. He moved into his Columbia office in June 1948.

During his years at Columbia, Eisenhower published his war memoirs, *Crusade in Europe.* He picked up his hobby of oil painting again as a way to relax. And Eisenhower and Mamie became grandparents. Dwight David II was born in 1948. John and Barbara would go on to have three more children: Barbara Anne, Susan, and Mary Jean.

Neither Eisenhower nor Mamie enjoyed Columbia very much. Mamie had never been to college, and she felt out of place with the sophisticated wives of the professors. Eisenhower also did not fit in well with the faculty. They did not feel that he was part of the academic community. They thought his strongest ties were still in Washington, D.C.

NATO

Eisenhower did maintain solid ties to Washington. In December 1948, he accepted a position as a military consultant to the Truman administration. He met with Department of Defense officials, testified on military issues before the Senate, and advised Truman.

In the spring of 1949, he took on an even bigger role. On April 4, the United States, Canada, and ten European nations signed the North Atlantic Treaty, forming a defense alliance. Hostilities between the Communist Soviet Union and democratic Europe and North America were increasing. The Cold War had begun. The North Atlantic Treaty Organization (NATO), as the alliance was called, was meant to guard Western European countries against Soviet aggression.

In October 1950, Truman asked Eisenhower to command the NATO forces. Eisenhower accepted, taking a leave of absence from Columbia.

Eisenhower was happy with the appointment to NATO. He told John, "I consider this to be the most important military job in the world." NATO headquarters were in Paris, so Eisenhower and Mamie moved there.

Eisenhower's task as NATO commander was to develop an army capable of stopping a Soviet advance into Western Europe. But his ability to carry out this task was limited. Still recovering from World War II, many Western European countries could contribute little to the NATO military force. The United States had the money and soldiers, but in June 1950, Communist North Korea invaded South Korea. U.S. troops intended for NATO had to be diverted to the Korean War.

Even in the face of setbacks, Eisenhower maintained his optimism about NATO. In 1951 he made a European broadcast: "I return with an unshakable faith in Europe . . . in the underlying courage of its people, in their willingness to live and sacrifice for a secure peace. . . ."

WE LIKE IKE

As another presidential election neared, several NATO supporters from the Republican Party approached Eisenhower about running. At the time, the party was dominated by a conservative senator from Ohio, Robert A. Taft. Taft was an isolationist who wanted to pull the United States out of NATO. Pro-NATO Republicans feared that Taft would get the party nomination if they could not find a strong candidate to run against him.

THE COLD WAR

The Communist Soviet Union was at odds politically with the capitalist democracies of Western Europe and the United States. In a Communist system, the government owns property and industries on behalf of the people. Leaders are not elected by citizens. The Communist Party is the only legal political group. In contrast, in democracies, citizens choose their leaders by voting. And in capitalism, private citizens own businesses, and the market for goods and services operates without excessive government control. But despite these political differences, the Soviet Union, Western Europe, and the United States had found a common enemy in Adolf Hitler and Nazi Germany. They had banded together to become the Allied forces in World War II.

After the war, however, the Allies fell back to old divisions. The Soviet Union resented Western influence. The Soviet government instead wanted to spread Communism to Eastern Europe and other developing countries. Western democracies, especially the United States, viewed the spread of Communism as a military threat and wanted to stop the Soviet Union.

Hostilities increased through the late 1940s and into the 1950s. The United States and Great Britain spied on the Soviet Union to monitor its military development, especially the development of nuclear missiles. The Soviet Union spied on the West for the same reason. Military reconnaissance planes routinely flew over enemy territory, taking photographs and gathering data. Agents infiltrated enemy organizations, stealing documents and recruiting foreign spies. Because these hostilities never heated up into an actual battle, the conflict was known as the Cold War. But a real war with nuclear weapons became a constant threat to people on both sides of the conflict.

Eisenhower did not want the United States to retreat back into isolation. He believed that at this point in history, it was the worst thing the country could do. The United States could serve as a strong deterrent against Cold War conflicts. Eisenhower began to think seriously about becoming a presidential candidate. But he was still a military officer, and according to military rules, he could not nominate himself. He had to be drafted for nomination by supporters.

John Hay Whitney, a New York millionaire, organized a rally of supporters on February 8, 1952. About 15,000 people stood in Madison Square Garden all night chanting, "We like Ike." A film of the rally was flown to Eisenhower in Paris, where he and Mamie watched in amazed silence. For Eisenhower, seeing regular people rallying for his nomination meant more than the coaxing and prodding of politicians. In April 1952, Eisenhower announced that he would seek the Republican nomination.

THE CANDIDATE

Eisenhower stood against Taft in the Republican primary elections. The winner of the primaries would get the Republican nomination. Eisenhower was an inexperienced campaigner, while Taft was a seasoned politician. But Eisenhower's popularity carried him to victory. After his victory, he asked to meet with Taft. It was unusual for the winner to reach out to the loser, but Eisenhower did not want to push Taft and his followers aside. He wanted to work with them to unify the party.

Immediately after the primaries, Eisenhower had to choose a running mate. A California senator named Richard Nixon had helped Eisenhower win the primary in

Eisenhower supporters chant, "We like Ike," and wave Ike signs during the 1952 Republican convention. Eisenhower won the Republican nomination for president.

that state. As a reward, some Republicans wanted Eisenhower to choose Nixon as a running mate. Eisenhower barely knew Nixon, and some of his aides strongly disliked the senator. But Eisenhower believed Nixon was his best choice. Nixon had a good military record in World War II and was strongly anti-Communist.

President Truman, a Democrat, decided not to run for reelection. In his place, the Democrats nominated Illinois governor Adlai E. Stevenson. The presidential campaign kicked into high gear.

Eisenhower's supporters had plenty of advice about what to do and say. He found himself skirting the issues and dodging questions. The campaign was designed to win votes, and every view had to be carefully expressed. It made Eisenhower uneasy.

Political opponents also began circulating rumors about Eisenhower's personal life. There were rumors that Mamie was an alcoholic, that Eisenhower had had a wartime affair with Kay Summersby, and that Eisenhower was hiding the fact that he was Jewish. Eisenhower was upset, but Truman tried to assure him: "If that's all it is, Ike, then you can just figure you're lucky."

WHISTLING THROUGH DIXIE

Early in the campaign, Eisenhower's advisers told him not to bother with the southern states. The South was Democrat country. Southerners would never vote Republican no matter what Eisenhower said, so there was no point in wasting campaign time there.

✧ ————————————

Candidate Eisenhower and wife, Mamie, wave to crowds from a train car during a campaign trip through the South.

Eisenhower decided against their advice. He organized a special whistle-stop campaign. He, Mamie, staff members, and reporters rode a train throughout the South. At train stations in cities and small towns, Republican organizers would gather a crowd together. Eisenhower's train would stop at the station, and he and Mamie would step out on the train's rear platform and speak to the people. Eisenhower also used the tour to meet with local Republican candidates. In the eight-week campaign, the Eisenhowers traveled more than 50,000 miles through forty-five states. He spoke in 232 towns.

The whistle-stop campaign was a success. The crowds liked Eisenhower's energy and confidence. His personality and simple way of talking about issues appealed to the crowds. Mamie was very popular too. She had no experience campaigning, but she had energy and personality to match her husband's.

CAMPAIGN ISSUES

As popular as Eisenhower was, he still faced all the criticisms and arguments that go along with any presidential campaign. One of his largest battles, however, was not against the Democrats but against groups within his own party. Isolationists wanted the United States to quit NATO and pull its troops out of Europe. Other groups wanted to limit unemployment benefits or abolish income tax.

Eisenhower was a moderate person who believed in cooperation. He did not want to split the Republican Party by either ignoring or giving in to a single group. He tried to take a middle ground. "I'm conservative where money is concerned, but liberal so far as human beings are concerned."

Likewise, he took a moderate position on other issues. He felt that the Korean War was being badly managed militarily and that the United States had to find a dignified way out of the conflict. On the issue of Cold War threats from Communist countries, he wanted the United States to remain strong militarily. But he urged against paranoia. He told audiences he did not like the way politicians exaggerated threats just to scare people. He argued that unity among the American people was the country's best defense.

Eisenhower campaign button
with the I Like Ike slogan
———— ✧ ————

Eisenhower campaigned up to the last minute. On Election Day 1952, he and Mamie took the train to New York, where they cast their ballots. Early returns showed a massive switch of Democrats to the Republican Party. When the final count was in, Eisenhower had 34 million votes to Stevenson's 27 million.

Eisenhower had won. Soon he would be the most powerful man in the free world.

CHAPTER SIX

THE FIRST TERM

The only way to win World War III
is to prevent it.

—Dwight D. Eisenhower

On the January day in 1953 when Eisenhower stepped up to the podium to give his inaugural address, he looked serious. Then his solemn expression gave way to his famous grin. His arms shot up over his head in a V-for-Victory sign. The crowd cheered. When it was quiet again, Eisenhower delivered his speech. He said the country's challenges were twofold: the dangers of war and of Communism. He promised that he would never stop seeking an honorable route to peace and freedom. The speech reflected the concerns of a postwar world.

A BID FOR PEACE

Soon after Eisenhower took office, Soviet leader Joseph Stalin died, on March 5, 1953. With the death of this dictator,

Outgoing president Harry S. Truman (left) wishes President Eisenhower (center) and Vice President Nixon (right) well on Inauguration Day 1953.

Eisenhower hoped the Soviet Union and the United States would have friendlier relations. In April he gave a famous speech called "The Chance for Peace."

In this speech, Eisenhower said, "The cost of one modern heavy bomber is this: a modern brick school in more than thirty cities. . . . It is two . . . fully equipped hospitals. We pay for a single fighter plane with a half-million bushels of wheat. We pay for a single destroyer [warship] with new homes that could have housed more than eight thousand people.

"This is not a way of life at all, in any true sense. Under the cloud of threatening war, it is humanity hanging from a cross of iron."

The president said that if the Soviet Union were ready for peace, the United States would begin reducing its supply of weapons and military equipment. By putting the ball in the Soviets' court, Eisenhower took a large step toward establishing the United States' leadership in the postwar world.

That leadership was enhanced when Eisenhower tackled the issue of U.S. involvement in the Korean War. During his campaign, Eisenhower had been vague about his ideas concerning Korea. During the summer of 1953, he took a much stronger position. The Communist government of China was supporting North Korean aggression against South Korea. Eisenhower warned the Chinese that he would take whatever steps necessary to end the conflict. Less than a decade after Hiroshima, the Chinese took the warning as a threat to use nuclear weapons and backed off. In July 1953, the North Koreans signed the treaty offered by the United States.

HOME ON PENNSYLVANIA AVENUE
While Eisenhower worked in the Oval Office, Mamie managed the entire White House. She oversaw a housekeeping staff that took care of 132 rooms. In a new age of international air travel, she and Eisenhower entertained an unprecedented number of heads of state. Over the years,

─────────────── ✧ ───────────────

The Eisenhowers met with many world leaders and dignitaries, including Britain's Queen Elizabeth (right center) *and Prince Philip* (left).

they hosted 70 kings, queens, prime ministers, and other leaders from all over the world.

Life in the White House was hectic, but Eisenhower was accustomed to long hours and hard work. Awake by 6:00 A.M. each day, he dressed and read the morning papers. He usually had breakfast with one guest, often his brother Milton. At 8:00 A.M., he walked through the White House to the Oval Office to read reports and letters. In the afternoon, he often took a break to hit golf balls on the White House lawn. On most days, he worked until 6:00 P.M. If no conferences were scheduled after dinner, he read reports or painted.

JOSEPH MCCARTHY

Eisenhower needed to keep on top of many issues in his daily reading and conferences. One of the most serious issues involved a U.S. senator. Since the early 1950s, Senator Joseph McCarthy, a Republican from Wisconsin, had made it his task to expose people he believed were Communist spies or Communist sympathizers within the U.S. government. There were Communist spies in the United States, just as there were American spies in the Soviet Union. The two superpowers watched each other's military developments very closely. But McCarthy had no evidence for most of his claims. He relied on Cold War fears to imply that anyone—a government official, a coworker, a favorite actress on TV—could be a Soviet agent working against the U.S. government.

Eisenhower was concerned about spying and national security, but he strongly disliked McCarthy's tactics. Yet, at first, Eisenhower chose to ignore the senator rather than

Senator Joseph McCarthy (center) *during one of his anti-Communist hearings of the 1950s. Eisenhower did not like the senator's actions.*

publicly denounce him. Anti-Communist investigations were popular with Republicans, and Eisenhower did not want to battle his own party. He also thought a public fight with McCarthy would only give the senator more publicity. Although Eisenhower's inaction was widely criticized, he would not change. It was only when McCarthy began making claims that the U.S. Army had Communist spies in positions of power that Eisenhower grew angry enough to act.

McCarthy claimed that he could prove Communists worked in the army. In the spring of 1954, he began a congressional hearing, televised nationally. He requested files for his investigations, but Eisenhower refused to hand them over. When McCarthy tried to put more pressure on him,

Eisenhower responded with executive privilege. That privilege ensures that advice given to the president by a government official is protected from congressional inquiry. Without the documents, McCarthy could not prove anything. McCarthy's bullying behavior also disgusted television audiences. His campaign to rid the country of Communists lost energy.

BROWN V. THE BOARD OF EDUCATION

Eisenhower faced another issue at home during his second year in office. The African American civil rights movement was growing. Since the Civil War (1861–1865), African Americans in the southern United States had lived under legal segregation. They lived, worked, and went to school separately from whites. In northern states, segregation was not legal, but African Americans were treated as second-class

———————————————— ✧ ————————————————

African American parents and children demonstrate for desegregation of public schools in the 1950s.

A mother and daughter sit on the steps of the U.S. Supreme Court, discussing the Court's 1954 decision that segregated schools were unconstitutional. The Supreme Court's ruling was a major victory for civil rights activists.

citizens. African Americans across the country began to organize themselves to battle these injustices. They wanted the basic rights guaranteed to everyone in the U.S. Constitution.

In May 1954, the U.S. Supreme Court ruled on a case called *Brown v. the Board of Education of Topeka.* Linda Brown, an African American teenager, lived in Topeka, Kansas. She had to attend an all-black public school, even though a white school was much closer to her home. Her father sued the school district to allow Linda to attend the white school. Chief Justice Earl Warren gave the Court's unanimous opinion on the case: racial segregation in public schools was unconstitutional. Schools across the South were ordered to desegregate immediately.

Eisenhower did not speak out in favor of the Court's ruling and did little to enforce it. He did not agree with segregation. But he believed that desegregation would take time and that social changes of this kind could not be forced by simply passing laws. But he could not ignore the growing civil rights movement.

VIETNAM

In foreign affairs, Eisenhower had to deal with war in the Southeast Asian country of Vietnam (then part of French Indochina). The Communist Viet Minh Army was fighting a bloody war against the French colonial government, and the Communists were winning. Eisenhower's secretary of state, John Foster Dulles, urged him to get involved. Leaders in the West did not want Vietnam to fall to the Communists, but Eisenhower refused to send in U.S. troops. He believed that U.S. troops would not fight well in Vietnam's jungles and too many soldiers would be killed. He also thought the intervention of more Westerners would only add to tensions in Asia.

The French surrendered to the Viet Minh in May 1954. Vietnam was divided into the Communist North and the anti-Communist South. After the French colonial government withdrew, the United States believed South Vietnam needed protection against a Communist takeover. South Vietnam was only a small country, but Eisenhower argued that it was important. He explained the situation in terms of a "domino effect." If dominoes are set up close together in a row and the first one gets knocked over, the rest will also fall. Eisenhower felt that in a similar way, if Communists took over South Vietnam, other countries in Southeast Asia would quickly fall to Communism. An entire region dominated by Communist countries could pose a threat to the United States and its allies. To protect South Vietnam, the United States established the Southeast Asia Treaty Organization (SEATO) in September 1954. Eisenhower also sent economic aid to South Vietnam. When Communist organizers began violent protests against the South Vietnamese government, Eisenhower sent military equipment and political advisers.

HEALTH PROBLEMS

In September 1955, while on vacation in Colorado, Eisenhower had serious health problems. He and his friend George Allen went out one afternoon to golf. Eisenhower wanted to relax, but he kept being called back to the club-house to take calls from Washington. He scored badly, his stomach hurt from his lunch of hamburgers with onions, and his temper was flaring. That evening, he went to bed early but woke in the middle of night with terrible chest pains.

Mamie called his doctor. He immediately gave Eisenhower some medicine and arranged for him to be transferred to a hospital. At sixty-five, the president had suffered a heart attack.

Two days after the attack, Eisenhower wanted to go back to work. But his doctors kept him in bed. Yet, if the president was not seen for a few days, it would be obvious to reporters that something was wrong. Eisenhower advised his press secretary to just tell people the truth.

After the press secretary announced Eisenhower's heart attack, the media rushed out the news. People across the world and across the United States were stunned. What was the president's real condition? Would he die?

A smiling President Eisenhower recovers at Fitzsimons Army Hospital, following a heart attack in September 1955.

✧ ——————

Mail began pouring into the hospital. After only a few days, thousands of get-well cards and letters had arrived. Mamie decided to reply to every well-wisher. John said, "I thought she was out of her mind." But while Eisenhower lay in bed regaining his strength, Mamie answered all the cards and letters by hand.

Once it became clear that Eisenhower was well enough to finish his term, people turned to another question: Would he run for office again? He was a popular leader, and the Republicans were counting on him to easily win another election. But Eisenhower did not want to commit to running again unless he knew he would be strong enough to endure the long hours and stress.

THE MONTGOMERY BUS BOYCOTT

Soon after Eisenhower's recovery, a civil rights crisis arose. On December 1, 1955, a black seamstress named Rosa Parks was riding a bus home from work in Montgomery, Alabama. According to Alabama's segregation laws, black bus riders had to give up their seats to whites on crowded buses. But that evening, when a white man demanded Mrs. Parks's seat, she refused to move. She was arrested. In protest, Montgomery's black community began a boycott. They refused to ride the city buses. The boycott was meant to last one day, but it continued for more than a year, until a federal court ordered Montgomery's buses to be desegregated.

Rosa Parks sits in the "for whites only" section of a Montgomery, Alabama, bus. Her dignified refusal to move out of the section sparked a citywide boycott of the segregated Montgomery bus system.

EISENHOWER'S AMERICA

Life in the United States changed so much after World War II that the 1950s became known as an era: Eisenhower's America. The period was characterized by both optimism and fear. Americans took pride in looking forward to the future. But it was also a time of uncertainty at home and abroad, and Americans sought comfort in traditional values of family life and hard work.

After World War II, the country saw the greatest period of economic growth in its history. The war created new industries, such as aviation and computers, providing hundreds of thousands of new jobs.

This prosperity in turn produced the most influential feature of postwar America, the Baby Boom. Many returning soldiers quickly settled down to family life. With new jobs and government loans for housing, Americans could afford to have more children. And they did. About 76 million babies were born in the United States from 1946 to 1964. The Baby Boom further stimulated the economy, creating a demand for new houses, schools, and many goods and services.

The emphasis on family life may be explained as a reaction to economic depression and war. People wanted assurance that those difficult times were over. Many moved to safe, comfortable new homes in the suburbs. Many people spent their money on cars, family vacations, and appliances. Advertisers recognized the huge market this new middle class represented.

As the postwar babies grew up, they created a whole new market too. Kids in the 1950s fashioned their own culture. They listened to a new kind of music called rock and roll. They sported their own styles of clothes and hairdos. And after their teenage years, they went off to college in record numbers, assuring themselves of continued success in American society.

Moviegoers wear 3-D (three-dimensional) glasses. Crazes such as 3-D movies were popular during the Eisenhower years.

But life in 1950s America was not all suburban prosperity. The Cold War created grave insecurity and fear. The development of the atomic weapons meant the conflict with the Soviet Union could escalate into massive destruction. Americans began building bomb shelters in their backyards, and schoolchildren practiced air-raid drills. Paranoia over Communist spies infiltrating American society sometimes reached the point of hysteria.

Domestic social issues also reached a boiling point. Not everyone shared in America's prosperity. Minorities, African Americans in particular, still faced poverty and discrimination. They began to demand basic rights in education, employment, and housing. But often their nonviolent demonstrations provoked violent reactions from whites opposed to integration. Even small steps forward, such as allowing a few African American students to attend a white school, had to be enforced by presidential orders and police escorts.

The boycott was the country's first large, organized protest against segregation. It was also the first time most of the country heard the name Martin Luther King Jr. King was a Baptist minister who had organized the boycott.

Again, Eisenhower failed to take a strong position in favor of civil rights actions like the boycott. But pressure was growing on him to take a stand.

LAST YEAR

In 1956, the last year of Eisenhower's term, he faced difficulties abroad and some triumphs at home. In the fall of 1956, students in Hungary demonstrated against their country's Communist government. In November Soviet leader Nikita Khrushchev sent in soldiers and tanks to crush the demonstrations. Hundreds of Hungarians were killed, and thousands were imprisoned or fled the country.

During his presidential campaign, Eisenhower had voiced commitment to freeing Eastern European countries from Soviet control. But in cases such as Hungary, he did not act to intervene. Eisenhower wanted to avoid clashing directly with the Soviet Union, since such a standoff could lead to nuclear war. He believed that Communism was a doomed system and that the Soviet Union would collapse when its own people rebelled. For Eisenhower, it was safer to wait.

Around the same time as the Soviet invasion of Hungary, a crisis was brewing in the Middle East over the Suez Canal. The canal runs through Egypt, connecting the Mediterranean and Red Seas. It is one of the busiest waterways in the world. Europe and Israel relied on being able to use it freely to ship oil. The British and French governments co-owned the company that operated the canal. But in July 1956, Egyptian president Gamal Nasser announced that Egypt would take complete control of the canal. Nasser wanted to free Egypt from foreign influence. In October, French, British, and Israeli troops responded by invading Egypt to regain control of the canal.

The invading countries expected the United States to support their attack, but Eisenhower refused. Eisenhower did not agree with Nasser's actions but was against the use of force. Without U.S. backing, the three countries had to withdraw.

FEDERAL-AID HIGHWAY ACT

In 1956 Eisenhower signed the Federal-Aid Highway Act. The act was the first move in creating the Interstate Highway System, the largest construction project in history. The act authorized the building of more than 43,000 miles of highway across the United States. The highway system had a military purpose—U.S. troops would be able to move quickly across the country if the mainland United States were ever attacked. But Eisenhower also believed that federal construction projects would help keep the economy strong by creating many jobs.

The highway system did create jobs in construction and manufacturing. But it had a much wider effect on both commercial and private activities. Since the highway system made travel easier, more people wanted to buy cars. That led to more growth in auto manufacturing and related industries such as steel, rubber, and oil. Other businesses and industries began to use interstate highways as a cheap, fast way to transport goods. Families began to take driving vacations,

A crew of workers builds a paved highway in South Carolina in the 1950s. Eisenhower pushed for the development of a national highway system.

────────────────── ✧ ──────────────────

and motels, roadside restaurants, and theme parks sprang up across the country.

CIVIL RIGHTS BILL

To end his term in office, Eisenhower sponsored a civil rights bill to protect African American voters in the South. African Americans who tried to register to vote were often harassed or turned away by local officials. The new bill stated that officials who interfered with voting rights could be taken to court. But at the last minute, a clause was added. It specified that the officials who violated the law would be tried by a jury. This clause greatly weakened Eisenhower's bill. Only registered voters are allowed to serve on juries. In the South, almost no African Americans were registered to vote. So most Southern juries would be completely white and unlikely to convict a white voting official. Eisenhower argued that only nonjury trials made sense, but his argument was defeated in the Senate by Lyndon B. Johnson of Texas.

REELECTION CAMPAIGN

By 1956 Eisenhower had fully recovered from his heart attack, and his doctors assured him he was in good health. He was ready to retire with Mamie to a farm they had bought in Pennsylvania. The Republican Party, however, feared that they would lose the 1956 election if anyone other than "Ike" ran. Eisenhower was not only a popular president, he was considered the most popular man in the country. Party officials convinced Eisenhower that he owed it to the country to continue the work he had started. He agreed and was nominated as the Republican candidate. The Democrats again nominated Adlai Stevenson. In this election, Eisenhower won by 9.5 million votes.

✧ ————————————

President Eisenhower raises his hands in victory on Election Night 1956. The president's win was a landslide.

CHAPTER SEVEN

THE SECOND TERM

The foundation for the American way of life is
our national respect for the law.
—Dwight D. Eisenhower

Immediately after his second term began, in January 1957, Eisenhower urged Congress to adopt a new doctrine under which the United States would pledge military and economic aid to any Middle Eastern country threatened by Communist aggression. The pledge became known as the Eisenhower Doctrine.

U.S. concerns about Communism continued. Communists were struggling to take control of the developing world. Decisions about U.S. defense spending and nuclear testing had to be made. Eisenhower wanted a secure country able to defend itself and a strong country able to defend others. He understood the need for military spending. But he worried greatly about creating a huge "military-industrial complex" paid for with government spending to create weapons.

He did not want military strength to overshadow diplomacy and peaceful developments in other areas of science and industry.

THE SPACE RACE

The United States was not the only country spending time and money on scientific and military technology. That fact became obvious on October 4, 1957, when the Soviet Union launched the world's first man-made satellite, called *Sputnik,* into space. Scientists all over the world marveled at it. The United States tried to counter by launching its own satellite. But it went up only a few hundred feet before crashing back to the launchpad. Newspapers sarcastically named the U.S. satellite "Kaputnik."

————————✧
The Soviets won the first lap of the space race by successfully launching the satellite Sputnik (right).

People in the United States were shocked at the news that the Soviets were ahead in the race to outer space. Why was the Soviet Union more advanced than the United States? The U.S. Army, Navy, and Air Force all blamed each other. Government engineers said they were not being paid enough. Democrats blamed Republicans, and Republicans blamed Democrats.

But for many people, the best explanation was that Soviet schools taught more math and science than U.S. schools. In the wake of the Sputnik embarrassment, Congress passed the National Defense and Education Act. The act provided loans to college students and grants to schools for improving education. Eisenhower was glad to see money going to colleges and schools, but he was uncomfortable viewing education as a defense strategy funded by the government.

LITTLE ROCK

While some American students dreamed of the space race, others dreamed of being able to go to school in peace. After *Brown v. the Board of Education,* schools in the South were required to start desegregating. Some schools refused to obey the law without a fight, and it was black students who were put on the front line of the battle.

In September 1957, Central High School in Little Rock, Arkansas, was ordered to desegregate. Nine African American students enrolled at Central, but when they tried to attend classes the first day, they were prevented from entering the school. White students and parents screamed obscenities and threw things at the African American teenagers. Arkansas' governor, Orval Faubus, called out the

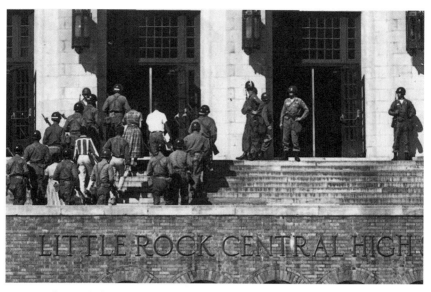

*Members of the 101st Airborne Division escort the Little Rock Nine
into Central High School in 1957.*

✧

Arkansas National Guard to block the doors. When Eisenhower heard this, he was outraged. A government official
had used a police force to disobey a federal order.

"There must be respect for the Constitution," he said,
"which means the Supreme Court's interpretation of the
Constitution, or we shall have chaos."

Eisenhower put the National Guard under federal control, which meant they had to obey him, not the governor.
Then he sent the army's 101st Airborne Division to protect
the African American students, who became known as the
Little Rock Nine.

Eisenhower proved correct when he said desegregation
would not be easily achieved by passing laws. The army
could get the Little Rock Nine into the school, but they

could not protect them from the rage and violence of students who did not want to share their school.

THE MIDDLE EAST

Throughout 1957, Eisenhower dealt with problems in the Middle East. The region was becoming increasingly unstable. Egypt's president Nasser had allied his country with the Soviets. The governments in Iraq, Lebanon, and Jordan were under attack from within.

In Asia, too, Communist Chinese attacked Taiwan and other nearby islands. Indonesia was close to falling to the Communists. Eisenhower sent U.S. troops to all these regions, but new problems occurred every day.

During this time, Eisenhower suffered another health setback. He was working at his desk on the afternoon of November 25, 1957, when he suddenly felt dizzy. He could not hold his pen nor read the words he had been writing. When he tried to stand, his head swam. His speech was slurred. His aides called White House doctors. After an examination, the doctors said Eisenhower had suffered a stroke.

After recovering, Eisenhower decided to test his strength by flying to Paris to meet with the heads of NATO. During the Paris meetings, Eisenhower found that he could hold his pen securely to write. He was not dizzy, and he spoke clearly. As he left, he shook hands with other heads of state. He had passed his test.

For a short while, his work went more smoothly. He had hopes of a breakthrough in the Cold War. In September 1959, Soviet leader Nikita Khrushchev visited the United States. Khrushchev traveled around the country and spoke at the United Nations, an international peace organization headquartered in New York City. Mamie and Nina Khrushchev, Nikita's wife, went shopping together. The Khrushchevs and the Eisenhowers relaxed at Camp David, the presidential retreat in Maryland named after the Eisenhowers' grandson. The two leaders decided to hold a summit meeting the next year in Paris with the leaders of Great Britain and France, to discuss strategies for easing the Cold War. Khrushchev, among other things, wanted better trade between the countries. Eisenhower wanted a treaty controlling nuclear weapons production. The summit was set for May 1960.

CASTRO

Soon after Eisenhower and Khrushchev made plans for a new peace, Communism landed just ninety miles off the coast of Florida. In January 1959, Fidel Castro seized power in Cuba. Castro soon began turning Cuba into a Communist country.

Communist leaders Fidel Castro (left) and Nikita Khrushchev (right). The alliance between Cuba and the Soviet Union threatened Soviet-American peace.

He took over U.S. businesses in Cuba and allied himself with the Soviet Union. He condemned the United States and spoke of spreading Communism throughout Central and South America.

Having a Communist government so close to the United States was an unacceptable threat. Eisenhower set up an economic blockade of Cuba, preventing Cuba from buying or selling goods in the United States. He also ordered the Central Intelligence Agency (CIA) to begin planning an invasion of Cuba to overthrow Castro.

U-2

Eisenhower's handling of Cuba pointed to a serious contradiction in Cold War strategies. Eisenhower planned to talk peace with Khrushchev while at the same time planning to destroy a Soviet ally. Khrushchev had his own inconsistencies. He supported Castro's condemnation of the United States while eagerly looking forward to the Paris summit. These contradictions caused a serious problem between the two countries as the Paris summit approached.

On May 1, 1960, just before the summit was to begin, Soviet troops shot down an airplane illegally flying over Soviet airspace. Khrushchev announced to his government assembly that it was an American U-2 spy plane. He denounced the "aggressive imperialist" act but did not blame Eisenhower. Instead, Khrushchev said he believed the CIA had planned the spying mission without Eisenhower's knowledge.

Eisenhower did know about the mission. But Khrushchev seemed to be leaving Eisenhower a chance to deal with the crisis diplomatically. Eisenhower, however, made the mistake of assuming that the plane had burned up and that the pilot

U.S.-Soviet relations were further strained when a U-2 spy plane (above) *was shot down over the Soviet Union in 1960.*

was dead. The Soviets would not be able to prove it was a spy mission. So Eisenhower publicly claimed that the U-2 was a weather plane that had simply flown off course. Khrushchev, in response, revealed that the Soviets had, in fact, captured the pilot, a CIA agent, "alive and kicking." They had also recovered parts of what was clearly a U-2.

Eisenhower was deeply embarrassed, but he would not apologize. The Soviet Union and the United States routinely spied on each other, so Khrushchev's outrage over U.S. imperialism was little more than political drama. Moreover, both men still intended to go to the Paris summit.

But hopes for the summit were not longstanding. At the first meeting, Khrushchev again launched into a tirade against U.S. spying, and Eisenhower again refused to apologize. When French president Charles de Gaulle and

British prime minister Harold Macmillan sided with Eisenhower, Khrushchev angrily abandoned the summit.

In many ways, the U-2 crisis was a classic Cold War battle. It was a minor incident that could have been easily and quietly defused. But no matter how much Khrushchev and Eisenhower both wanted to make history by ending the Cold War, neither would back down over the U-2 affair. In the face of fear and mistrust, each had to make a show of power.

For Eisenhower, the collapse of the Paris summit seemed the worst event of his presidency. At the height of the U-2 crisis, he had wanted to resign. After the failed summit, he felt all he had come away with was another lost chance for peace.

THE END OF AN ERA

For whatever failures Eisenhower felt responsible, a vast majority of Americans still trusted and admired him. He left office as popular as ever. Some historians believe he could have easily won another election, if presidents were not limited to two terms.

In his farewell address to the nation on January 17, 1961, he spoke of the future of the country he had served for fifty years:

> *America today is the strongest, the most influential and most productive nation in the world. Understandably proud of this pre-eminence, we yet realize that America's leadership and prestige depend, not merely upon our unmatched material progress, riches and military strength, but on how we use our power in the interests of world peace and human betterment.*

EPILOGUE

When I was a small boy growing up in Kansas, a friend of mine and I . . . talked about what we wanted to do when we grew up. I told him I wanted to be a real major league baseball player. . . . My friend said that he'd like to be president of the United States. Neither of us got our wish.

—Dwight D. Eisenhower

During the last months in the White House, Mamie had been preparing to move to their farm in Gettysburg, Pennsylvania. The farm had several hundred acres for hay, corn, oats, barley, soybeans, and sorghum. From their house, Eisenhower and Mamie could see their green pastures and prize Angus cattle.

John was retired from the army. He, Barbara, and their children lived nearby. Eisenhower kept horses for his grandchildren to ride and dogs for them to play with.

On the farm, Eisenhower spent more time with his hobby of oil painting. And during the winter, he and Mamie stayed in Palm Desert, California, where he could golf every day.

MAMIE

Mamie Geneva Doud was born in November 11, 1896, in Boone, Iowa. She was the second of four daughters born to John and Elivera Doud. John made a small fortune in the meatpacking business and retired young. When Mamie was seven, the family moved to Denver, Colorado. By all accounts, Mamie's childhood was very happy. Her family was warm, talkative, and loved to have fun.

Mamie Doud Eisenhower, 1950s

Like many young women of her generation and social class, Mamie was never raised to go to college or have a career. She finished high school and began dating young men with a view toward getting married. But Mamie was never just another pretty debutante. She was bright and witty, with a teasing sense of humor. She was also, her granddaughter Susan noted, a confident, no-nonsense type. And perhaps that is why many of Denver's eligible bachelors bored Mamie. And perhaps that is why she found the gruff, rebellious soldier named Eisenhower so appealing.

Throughout Eisenhower's military and political careers, Mamie offered support and advice. As a military wife, she moved the Eisenhower household thirty-five times in thirty-seven years. Her own plans and wishes often took a backseat to the demands of the military. But she understood Eisen-hower's commitment to the job, and she was always confident of his commitment to his family.

When Eisenhower entered politics, Mamie was thrust into the spotlight too. She was not a political person, but on the campaign trail, Eisenhower's aides found that Mamie "had a real rapport with the crowds and was a good sport with the news media." Supporters began carrying posters that read, "I Like Ike, But I LOVE Mamie."

Her popularity carried over to her time as First Lady. Mamie welcomed dignitaries from around the world. She was warm and relaxed—famous for being able to put White House guests at ease. Like her husband, Mamie was one of America's most admired and popular public figures.

A book publisher offered $1 million for his presidential memoirs, so he began to write. Eventually, he published three books. Two were presidential histories, *Mandate for Change* (1963) and *Waging Peace* (1965). The third, called *At Ease: Stories I Tell to Friends* (1967), was a personal memoir of his childhood in Abilene, his life with Mamie, and his time in the U.S. Army.

Eisenhower stayed involved in politics too, after Democrat John F. Kennedy was elected president after him. Eisenhower had been bitterly disappointed that the Democrats had taken office again. But when Kennedy needed advice on Castro and Cuba, Eisenhower was there

to help him. He also later advised President Lyndon Johnson, who came to office in 1963. In 1968 Eisenhower supported his former vice president,

✧ ———————————

Eisenhower takes a break from his painting to have his picture taken in the 1950s. Throughout his presidency and his retirement, Eisenhower found painting relaxing.

Richard Nixon, in his bid for the presidency. Nixon won. That same year, Eisenhower's grandson David married Nixon's daughter Julie.

After leaving the White House, Eisenhower had health problems, including more heart attacks. By March 1969, his heart was failing, and he was moved to Walter Reed Army Hospital. Mamie stayed in the room next to his.

On March 28, Eisenhower took a turn for the worse. His family gathered around his bed to say good-bye. He told them all that he loved them. Then Mamie held his hand as he passed away.

After a military funeral attended by the world's leaders, Eisenhower was buried in Abilene. At the end of his journey from soldier to president, he returned to his home on the Kansas plains.

TIMELINE

1890 David Dwight Eisenhower is born on October 14 in Denison, Texas.

1911 Eisenhower is appointed to the U.S. Military Academy at West Point.

1915 Eisenhower graduates from West Point.

1916 Eisenhower is commissioned as a second lieutenant in the U.S. Army. He meets and marries Mamie Doud.

1917 Eisenhower is promoted to captain and assigned to training duty. The Eisenhowers' first son, Doud, is born.

1921 Doud dies of scarlet fever.

1922 The Eisenhowers' son John is born. Eisenhower is assigned to the Panama Canal Zone in Central America.

1926 Eisenhower graduates from the army's Command and General Staff School at Fort Leavenworth, Kansas. He is appointed as an aide to General John J. Pershing.

1928 Eisenhower graduates from the Army War College.

1935 Eisenhower accompanies General Douglas MacArthur to the Philippines.

1941 In December the United States enters World War II.

1942 Eisenhower is sent to London to command the U.S. Army's European Theater of Operations. In November he leads Operation Torch, the invasion of North Africa.

1943 Eisenhower is chosen to lead Operation Overlord, the invasion of German-occupied France. He is named Supreme Commander of the Allied Expeditionary Forces.

1944 On June 6, Allied forces invade the coast of Normandy. In December Eisenhower is promoted to the U.S. Army's highest rank, general of the army.

1945 Germany surrenders at Reims, France. Eisenhower becomes commander of the American occupation forces in Germany.

1948 Eisenhower retires from the army as a five-star general. He becomes president of Columbia University in New York City.

1950 President Harry Truman appoints Eisenhower commander of North Atlantic Treaty Organization (NATO) troops.

1952 Eisenhower begins his campaign for the U.S. presidency.

1953 Eisenhower is sworn in as the thirty-fourth U.S. president.

1954 The U.S. Supreme Court's decision in *Brown v. the Board of Education* outlaws racial segregation in public schools.

1955 Eisenhower is reelected president by a wide margin of votes.

1956 Eisenhower sponsors a civil rights bill reinforcing the voting rights of Southern blacks.

1957 Eisenhower orders the National Guard to Central High School in Little Rock, Arkansas, to enforce a desegregation order.

1959 Fidel Castro comes to power in Cuba. Eisenhower orders a ban on trade to Cuba.

1960 A U.S. spy plane shot down over Soviet territory scuttles a peace summit with Soviet leader Nikita Khrushchev.

1961 Eisenhower delivers his farewell address to the American people before leaving office. He and Mamie retire to a farm in Pennsylvania.

1969 On March 28, Eisenhower dies in Washington, D.C.

SOURCE NOTES

10 John McCallum, *Six Roads from Abilene: Some Personal Recollections of Edgar Eisenhower* (Seattle: Wood and Reber, 1960), 19–20, quoted in Carlo D'Este, *Eisenhower: A Soldier's Life* (New York: Henry Holt, 2002), 32.

14 Kenneth Davis, *Soldier of Democracy* (Garden City, NY: Doubleday, Doran, 1945), 32–33, quoted in Geoffrey Perret, *Eisenhower* (New York: Random House, 1999), 22.

14 Dwight D. Eisenhower, *At Ease: Stories I Tell to Friends* (Garden City, NY: Doubleday, 1967), 94.

15 Ibid., 52.

18 Relman Morin, *Dwight D. Eisenhower* (New York: Simon and Schuster, 1969), 18.

20 Eisenhower, *At Ease,* 4.

23 Ibid.

23 *United States Military Academy at West Point,* "Center for Professional Military Ethic," n.d., <http://www.usma.edu/Cpme> (September 2003).

24 Eisenhower, *At Ease,* 20.

26 Susan Eisenhower, *Mrs. Ike: Memories and Reflections on the Life of Mamie Eisenhower* (New York: Farrar, Straus and Giroux, 1996), 31.

29 Eisenhower, *At Ease,* 29.

30 Stephen E. Ambrose, *Eisenhower: Soldier and President* (New York: Simon and Schuster, 1990), 30.

32 Eisenhower, *Mrs. Ike,* 45.

33 Morin, *Dwight D. Eisenhower,* 33.

34 Lt. Ed Thayer to his mother, November 1, 1918, Eisenhower Library, quoted in Ambrose, *Eisenhower: Soldier and President,* 32.

42 Ambrose, *Eisenhower: Soldier and President,* 48.

43 D'Este, *Eisenhower: A Soldier's Life,* 705.

50 Ambrose, *Eisenhower: Soldier and President,* 142.

51 John M. Stagg, *Forecast for Overlord* (London: I. Allan, 1971), 104–109, quoted in Perret, *Eisenhower,* 281.

52 Ambrose, *Eisenhower: Soldier and President,* 140.

54 D'Este, *Eisenhower: A Soldier's Life,* 644.

54 Ambrose, *Eisenhower: Soldier and President,* 175.

56 Dwight D. Eisenhower, *The Papers of Dwight D. Eisenhower,* vol. 4, ed. Albert D. Chandler, et al. (Baltimore: Johns Hopkins Press, 1970), 2696, quoted in Perret, *Eisenhower,* 348.

56 George C. Marshall to Dwight Eisenhower, May 8, 1945, Eisenhower, *The Papers of Dwight D. Eisenhower,* quoted in Ambrose, *Eisenhower: Soldier and President,* 201–202.

57 Dwight D. Eisenhower, *Crusade in Europe* (Garden City, NY: Doubleday, 1948), 444, quoted in Perret, *Eisenhower,* 352.

58 Dwight D. Eisenhower, *Letters to Mamie,* ed. John S. D. Eisenhower (Garden City, NY: Doubleday, 1978), 254, in Ambrose, *Eisenhower: Soldier and President,* 205.

59 Eisenhower, *At Ease,* 389.

59 Ambrose, *Eisenhower: Soldier and President,* 207.

64 Eisenhower to Neill Bailey, August 1, 1945, Eisenhower, *The Papers of Dwight D. Eisenhower,* quoted in Ambrose, *Eisenhower: Soldier and President,* 208.

64 Perret, *Eisenhower,* 351.

64 Dwight D. Eisenhower, *The Eisenhower Diaries,* ed. Robert H. Ferrel (New York: W. W. Norton, 1981), 162.

66 Dwight D. Eisenhower, Eisenhower Diary, July 6, 1950, Eisenhower Library, quoted in Ambrose, *Eisenhower: Soldier and President,* 250.

66 Eisenhower, *At Ease,* 366.

70 Peter Lyon, *Eisenhower: Portrait of the Hero* (Boston: Little Brown, 1974), 439, quoted in Ambrose, *Eisenhower: Soldier and President,* 268.

71 Perret, *Eisenhower,* 413.

73 Dwight D. Eisenhower in Public Broadcasting System/WGBH, "Dwight D. Eisenhower," *The American Experience: The Presidents,* 1993, <http://www.pbs.org/wgbh/amex/presidents/34_eisenhower/index.html> (October 2003).

74 Dwight D. Eisenhower, Public Papers of the President of the United States (53), quoted in Ambrose, *Eisenhower: Soldier and President,* 326.

82 John Eisenhower, *Strictly Personal* (Garden City, NY: Doubleday, 1974), 181.

90 Morin, *Dwight D. Eisenhower,* 132.

90 Dwight D. Eisenhower, "Farewell Address to the Nation, January 17, 1961," *Eisenhower's Farewell Address to the Nation,* n.d., <http://mcadams.posc.mu.edu/ike.htm> (September 2003).

93 Dwight D. Eisenhower, letter, Swede Hazlett, quoted in Ambrose, "Dwight D. Eisenhower," *Character Above All: An Exploration of Presidential Leadership,* Public Broadcasting System, n.d. <http://www.pbs.org/newshour/character/essays/eisenhower.html> (October 2003).

96 *New York Times,* May 6, 1960, quoted in Ambrose, *Eisenhower: Soldier and President,* 508.

97 *New York Times,* May 8, 1960, quoted in Ambrose, *Eisenhower: Soldier and President,* 510.

98 Eisenhower, "Farewell Address to the Nation."

99 Dwight D. Eisenhower, "Dwight D. Eisenhower, 1890–1969," *Brainy Quote: Famous Quotes and Quotations,* n.d., <http://www. brainyquote.com /quotes/authors/ d/dwightdei126839 .html> (September 2003).

101 Eisenhower, *Mrs. Ike,* 272.

101 Ibid., 274.

SELECTED BIBLIOGRAPHY

Ambrose, Stephen E. *D-Day: June 6, 1944: The Climactic Battle of World War II.* New York: Touchstone Books, 1995.

————. *Eisenhower: Soldier and President.* New York: Simon and Schuster, 1990.

D'Este, Carlo. *Eisenhower: A Soldier's Life.* New York: Henry Holt, 2002.

Eisenhower, Dwight D. *At Ease: Stories I Tell to Friends.* Garden City, NY: Doubleday, 1967.

————. *The Eisenhower Diaries.* Edited by Robert H. Ferrell. New York: W. W. Norton, 1981.

Eisenhower, John. *Strictly Personal.* Garden City, NY: Doubleday, 1974.

Eisenhower, Susan. *Mrs. Ike: Memories and Reflections on the Life of Mamie Eisenhower.* New York: Farrar, Straus and Giroux, 1996.

Morin, Relman. *Dwight D. Eisenhower.* New York: Simon and Schuster, 1969.

Perret, Geoffrey. *Eisenhower.* New York: Random House, 1999.

Stassen, Harold, and Marshall Houts. *Eisenhower: Turning the World toward Peace.* St. Paul, MN: Merrill/Magnus Publishing, 1990.

Sulzberger, C. L., and Stephen E. Ambrose. *American Heritage New History of World War II.* New York: Viking Press, 1997.

United States Military Academy. *United States Military Academy at West Point.* N.d. <www.usma.edu> (October 2003).

Weiss, Jessica. *To Have and to Hold: Marriage, the Baby Boom, and Social Change.* Chicago: University of Chicago Press, 2000.

Wicker, Tom. *Dwight D. Eisenhower.* New York: Henry Holt, 2002.

Further Reading and Websites

Adler, David A. *A Picture Book of Dwight David Eisenhower.* New York: Holiday House, 2002.

The American Experience: The Presidents. <http://www.pbs.org/wgbh/amex/presidents/index.html>. Visitors can access biographies of U.S. presidents, including Dwight D. Eisenhower. Features of the Eisenhower pages include fun facts about the president and an interactive vote on issues Eisenhower faced as president.

The Dwight Eisenhower Library and Museum. <http://www.eisenhower.utexas.edu>. This official website of the Eisenhower Library chronicles the life and politics of Dwight D. Eisenhower.

Eisenhower Birthplace State Historical Park. <http://www.eisenhowerbirthplace.org>. Highlights of this site include Eisenhower's paintings, his family tree, photographs of his Texas home, and research links to information about the president.

Finlayson, Reggie. *We Shall Overcome: The History of the American Civil Rights Movement.* Minneapolis: Lerner Publications Company, 2003.

Goldstein, Margaret J. *World War II—Europe.* Minneapolis: Lerner Publications Company, 2004.

Kallen, Stuart A., ed. *The 1950s.* San Diego: Lucent Books, 1999.

Lazo, Caroline Evensen. *Harry S. Truman.* Minneapolis: Lerner Publications Company, 2003.

Marling, Karal Ann. *As Seen on TV: The Visual Culture of Everyday Life in the 1950s.* Cambridge, MA: Harvard University Press, 1996.

Márquez, Herón. *Richard M. Nixon.* Minneapolis: Lerner Publications Company, 2003.

Sherman, Josepha. *The Cold War.* Minneapolis: Lerner Publications Company, 2004.

Welch, Catherine A. *Children of the Civil Rights Era.* Minneapolis: Carolrhoda Books, 2001.

Williams, Barbara. *World War II—The Pacific.* Minneapolis: Lerner Publications Company, 2005.

INDEX

ABOUT THE AUTHOR

Jean Darby has published more than sixty books and numerous newspaper articles. Her children's books include how-to-read and picture books, science and social studies books, and biographies. In addition to *Dwight D. Eisenhower*, Darby has written biographies of Douglas MacArthur and Martin Luther King Jr. She also taught elementary school and was a college creative writing instructor. She lives with her family in northern California.

---------- ✧ ----------